IMAGES OF ENGLAND

J.B. PRIESTLEY'S
BRADFORD

IMAGES OF ENGLAND

J.B.PRIESTLEY'S BRADFORD

GARY FIRTH

TEMPUS

Frontispiece: Mr J.B. Priestley, the successful author of *The Good Companions*.

First published 2006

Tempus Publishing Limited
The Mill, Brimscombe Port,
Stroud, Gloucestershire, GL5 2QG
www.tempus-publishing.com

British Library Cataloguing in Publication Data.
A catalogue record for this book is available from the British Library.

ISBN 0 7524 3865 4

Typesetting and origination by Tempus Publishing Limited.
Printed in Great Britain.

Contents

Acknowledgements

A number of people have contributed to the images in this book and to the original exhibition at the J.B. Priestley Library of the University of Bradford. I am indebted to three principal sources:

Firstly, to Tom Priestley for allowing me to use personal family photographs from the Priestley archive at the University of Bradford. Also thanks to Alison Cullingford, senior curator of that collection, for permission to access family letters and other correspondence.

Secondly, I owe a huge debt of gratitude to David Pratt for permission to use images from the private collection of his grandfather Christopher Pratt, a schoolboy contemporary of Priestley's at Belle Vue School.

Lastly, my thanks go to the Bradford Libraries and Museum services and the *Bradford Telegraph and Argus* for permission to use photographs in their respective collections.

Other contributors include David Burnet, Dorothy Burrows, Graham Hall, Gordon Hodgson, Malcolm Hitt, Dorothy Firth and Frank Woodall.

Thanks go to those anonymous photographers of years gone by whose efforts have survived to embellish this publication.

If any copyrights have been infringed, there has been no deliberate intent and for anyone whose help has not been acknowledged the fault is entirely that of the author, as are any factual errors in the text.

Finally a special thank you to Ian Ward for photographic expertise and to Marlene Sharkey for secretarial assistance.

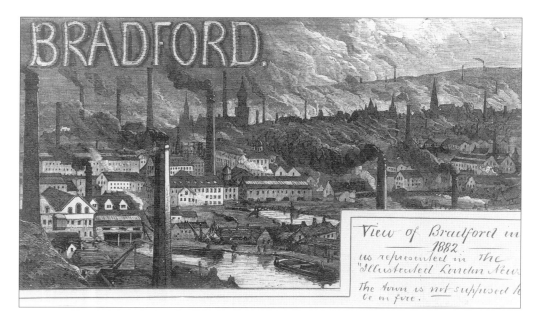

Foreword by Tom Priestley

My father was born in Manningham, Bradford in September 1894 and left that city to fight on the Western Front at the age of twenty, never again to reside permanently in the place of his birth. Yet he has left his mark upon that proud northern town.

In 1929 the Bradford Civic Theatre was founded by a group of theatre-lovers headed by his stepmother. My father became its first president as the Bradford Playhouse became one of the leading amateur theatres in the country. Now known as the Priestley, it flourishes still. A University of Bradford Library also takes his name and there, in 1997, was established a permanent exhibition of the same title as this book.

Gary Firth's research and collection of images for that exhibition are the origins of this publication, which I am pleased to commend to both historians and devotees of J.B. Priestley's writings.

Here, from the words of my father and from evocative images of contemporary photographers, Dr Firth takes us back, like time travellers, into the high Edwardian era.

Each of you may have your own Bradford but this is my father's and he presides over it permanently from his plinth overlooking the city centre.

One could imagine a Bradford without him but never J.B. Priestley without Bradford.

Tom Priestley
London, November 2005

Right: A very young Jack Priestley, *c.* 1895.

Opposite: A view of Bradford in 1882 as featured in the *Illustrated London News.*

Introduction

J.B. PRIESTLEY'S BRADFORD, 1894

If ever a writer was moulded and fashioned by the environment into which he or she was born and nurtured, it was J.B. Priestley in the West Riding of Yorkshire before 1914, more particularly in the Bradford of the Edwardian era. He once said of his two most biographical works: 'if there are better accounts of what it was like to be a youngster in pre-1914 Bradford than there are in *Bright Day* and *Margin Released*, I would dearly like to read them.'

He was always of the opinion that a person's formative years were not those of childhood but those of one's teenage years, from the age of fifteen to nineteen and for Priestley, born in 1894, that placed him at the heart of the Edwardian era. It is no coincidence that he wrote a book entitled *The Edwardians* and that he often regarded himself as being 'an Edwardian'.

As early as 1931, in the *Heaton Review*, he informed his Bradford suburban readership:

> *Bradford where I was born and where I lived the most exciting and perhaps the most important years of my life. To me, Bradford is not one manufacturing town out of many, a place to be visited and sketched; it is not really a town at all, it is a vast series of pictures in time and space; it is an autobiographical library; it is a hundred thousand succeeding states of mind, it is my childhood and youth; it is a lost world.*

In this publication we take a peep into the Bradford way of life during the years before the First World War. Through a selection of photographic images and some of Priestley's own written words I hope that you the reader are able to share a vivid, if transient, understanding of a great writer's 'lost world'. And so it was, for Priestley's early life coincided with the zenith of Bradford's golden age as a classic nineteenth-century provincial town. It was a unique experience in urban history and to one of its favourite sons a very special place indeed. In a preface of the biography of a Bradford socialist in 1946 Priestley wrote:

> *The Bradford of those years was no ordinary city ... In those pre-1914 days Bradford was considered the most progressive place in the United Kingdom .... I am prepared to bet that Bradford produced more well known people – musicians, scientists, writers, performers and the like than any place, anything like its size, in the whole kingdom.*

PRIESTLEY'S HOME TOWN

The nineteenth century was the age of the great provincial towns and, by 1894, Bradford had become one of the most notable northern cities, growing from a small market town in 1801 (township population 6,393) to the seventh largest community in Britain fifty years later. That growth had its foundations in an expanding and prosperous worsted trade, employing thousands of the city's workforce.

By the time of Jack Priestley's birth in 1894, Bradford had become a watchword for urban decline, poor quality housing and declining standards of public health. The view of Bradford from an article in the *Illustrated London News* of 1882 compels the editor of that journal to explain to his southern readership that the town is not actually on fire. In fact, since the

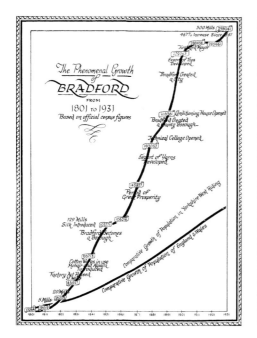

Top left: Comparative graphs showing Bradford's population growth 1801-1931.

Top right: Heritage plaque at 34 manheim Road, Bradford, birthplace of J.B. Priestley.

Above: A bradford colliery at Wyke.

incorporation of the town in 1847 there had been a slow but quantative improvement in Bradford's social, civic and economic infrastructures. In 1877 the corporation undertook a widespread programme of slum clearance, particularly of the notorious cellar dwellings and of the huddled, unhygienic courts and yards of the 1840s.

The decade of steady economic growth and municipal reinvestment after 1850 was followed by fifteen years of prosperity and unprecedented civic achievement. As a result, the class

A view of the main street and mill of the model village of Titus Salt's Saltaire in 1887.

conflict which had characterised the 1840s gave way to social harmony as working-class radicals were drawn into the ranks of Liberalism or were won over by the doctrines of self-help and self-improvement by means of education and the chapel.

A few mill owners and employers like Titus Salt at Saltaire adopted a more paternalistic and conciliatory approach to industrial relations. This only worked well as long as profits were high and business was brisk. Although Bradford and its many mill owners continued to thrive in the English worsted trade (to the extent that the town took up its name of 'Worstedopolis'), overseas competition, low capital investment, and changes of fashion all loomed on the commercial horizon by 1894 and threatened the security and social stability of Bradford's mid-Victorian years. The result was that a new generation of employers took a less altruistic line with their employees than had their fathers and grandfathers, which in turn, sharpened the political consciousness of the town's skilled textile workers as well as the growing ranks of semi-skilled operatives in the local engineering shops, dye houses, iron works and collieries. All of whom had been armed with the vote since the 1867 Reform Act.

In addition, at this time of growing political awareness, the traditional heartland of industrial Bradford was being vacated by a population growth that was beginning to slow down and to redistribute, as thousands of artisans and middle-class families fled like lemmings to the new suburbs of Bradford Moor, Heaton and Allerton. It was into one of Bradford's more salubrious suburbs, Manningham, that Jack Priestley was born on 13 September 1894 at 34 Mannheim Road, off Toller Lane.

one

A Bradford Boyhood

PRIESTLEY FAMILY TREE

JOHN PRIESTLEY married **MARY**
BORN BRADFORD 1832   BORN BRADFORD 1826
COTTON WARP DRESSER   HOUSEWIFE

ALLAN	**JONATHAN**	GEORGE	ANNIE	SARAH
Cotton Warp	School Teacher	Joiner &	Cotton Warp	b.1871
Twister		Builder	Teaser	unmarried
unmarried		one daughter	unmarried	
		CONSTANCE		
		d.1995		

HOLT married SARAH
b.1801

THOMAS married ANN
b. 1833, Yorkshire   b. 1837, Ireland
Stoker in Silk Mill   Silk Picker
d. before 1881

MARY ANN	ELIZA	SARAH	**EMMA**	JOSEPH	HY?	THOS	ANNIE
b.1858	b.1860	b.1863	b.1865	b.1868	b.1871	b.1874	b.1876
d.before	Silk	Velvets	**Silk**	Silk	d. before		
1881	Spinner	Weaver	**Spinner**	Spinner	1881		

JONATHAN PRIESTLEY married EMMA HOLT
4th August 1891, St John's Chapel
JOHN (JACK) born 13th September 1894
EMMA died 17th October 1896, interred at Heaton
JONATHAN married AMY FLETCHER 1898
WINNIE born 15th November 1903

JACK (now **JOHN BOYNTON**) married EMILY 'PAT' TEMPEST, 29th July 1921
JONATHAN died Summer 1924
PAT died Autumn 1925

J.B.P. married WINIFRED JANE WYNDHAM LEWIS nee HOLLAND
September 1926, divorced 1952
J.B.P. married JACQUETTA HAWKES, July 1953
J.B. PRIESTLEY died 14th August 1984

Priestley family tree. Jack Priestley (henceforth JBP) is firmly rooted in the working-class tradition of Bradford's textile industry. Both sets of his grandparents had worked in the mill. Grandfather John Priestley worked as a cotton warp dresser in the 1850s, and Thomas Holt (maternal side) was a stoker at Manningham Mills.

LISTER & CO. LTD.

SILK SPINNERS, MANUFACTURERS DYERS & FINISHERS

MANNINGHAM MILLS   BRADFORD, ENGLAND

PILE FABRICS AND TAPESTRIES:

"LISVEL" (Regd.)	"LISPLUS" (Regd.)	"LISANGO" (Regd.)
Black and Colored Velvets, Antique Velvets, Chiffon Velvets, etc., for Dresses and Millinery.	Plain, Figured, Ombre and Embossed Silk Plushes, for Dresses, Millinery and Fancy Goods.	Mohair Utrecht Velvet, plain and embossed, Genoa and Broche Velvets, Frisé Velvets, Moquettes, etc.
"LISREINE" (Regd.)	"LISFUR" (Regd.) *(Silk & Mohair Pile).*	"LISKURL" (Regd.) *(Curl Centre).*
Rich Silk Seals, rainproofed by special process. *Wholesale only.*	Seals, Beavers, Fox, Ermine, Mole, Chinchilla, Squirrel, Caracules, Imitation Pony and Bear, etc., etc. *Wholesale only.*	Mats, Rugs, Table Covers, Church Seatings, Curtain Cloths, Car Seatings, etc., etc.

TAPESTRIES *for all purposes.*   We manufacture a large variety of Tapestries in Silk, Mohair, Worsted, Cotton, Artificial Silk, etc., and combinations of these materials.

FOR LIST OF DEPÔTS, SEE END OF BOOK.

Manningham Mills were, at that time, Bradford's largest and best-equipped factory, built as late as 1873 by S.C. Lister and famous for their silk and velvet cloths.

Right: Emma Holt (born in 1865) was one of eight children of Thomas and Ann Holt. Like her mother and three of her sisters, Emma worked in the spinning department at Manningham Mills.

Below: Lilycroft Road/Silk Street, Manningham, *c.* 1890. This tranquil scene in the streets around the mill at Manningham was violently disturbed in April 1891 when Lister and his board of directors tried to offset the harmful American tariff on cloth exports by drastic wage cuts. Angry workers picketed the mill but large public meetings in Bradford centre were forcibly broken up by police and armed troops.

JBP's parents on honeymoon at Blackpool, August 1891. Young Emma Holt was too preoccupied with her forthcoming marriage to a local schoolteacher to care about reduced wages and the betrayal of the local working-class Trades Council by the Bradford Liberal group.

Westgate Baptist Chapel (St John's). On 4 August 1891 Emma Holt walked proudly down the aisle of this nonconformist chapel, the regular place of worship for her husband Jonathan Priestley.

Jonathan Priestley – JBP's father came from an altogether different background than his mother. Jonathan (b. 1868) belonged to the respectable upwardly mobile ranks of the Bradford artisan class. His father had risen to the position of overlooker at the mill and had been able to save enough money to send his second son to teacher training college whence he returned to work in Bradford's progressive School Board system. In 1962 J.B. Priestley wrote of his father, 'he had plucked my mother, my real mother about whom I knew nothing except that she was high-spirited and witty, from the "clogs and shawls back o'mill", a free and easy raffish kind of working-class life.'

Staff at Belle Vue Board School, Bradford, c. 1895. As a young class teacher Jonathan Priestley was inevitably influenced by the poverty of many of his pupils and as a committed chapel-goer he was not oblivious of the poor social and working conditions around him. By the time of this photograph (Priestley stands top left on the back row) he sympathised with the demand for independent working-class political representation in the aftermath of the terrible events at Manningham in 1891. On the row in front of him (high collar) stands Richard Pendlebury, a future major influence upon his son Jack.

23. August. 1894.

Registration Examined :~
Walter Ackroyd.

Aug. 28. Mr Shepherdson absent to-day through
illness.

Sept. 11th Mr Priestley absent this afternoon.

Report of H. M. Inspector . 1893-4.
This School is "ably conducted, and
the quality of the elementary work
is thoroughly good, being accurate
and intelligent throughout. The
singing and music are excellent; if

Extract from Belle Vue School logbook, September 1894. This entry by the Headmaster Mr Lishman of Belle Vue School shows Jonathan Priestley absenting himself from classes for the afternoon of 11 September 1894 to walk (as was his custom twice daily) the two miles to his home where his wife of two years was in labour with their first child. Two days later John Priestley was born and known henceforth by family and friends as 'Jack'.

34 Mannheim Road, birthplace of J.B. Priestley. By the 1890s row upon row of solid stone-built terraced houses were beginning to make up Bradford's suburban sprawl and it was in one of the town's wealthier suburbs, Manningham, that Jack Priestley was born. It was here also that Emma Priestley suffered a long and painful illness of ovarian cancer following JBP's birth. She died in October 1896 and was interred at Heaton. The silence in the little terraced house was broken only by the comings and goings of an ambitious schoolteacher and the crying of a two-year-old toddler whose 'dark bewilderment' was broken only by the emotional sustenance of a housekeeper and an Irish grandmother.

Right: Amy Fletcher in 1936. Two years later in August 1898 Jonathan Priestley married for a second time, to Amy Fletcher who worked in a nearby confectioner's shop. She immediately gave up her job to move into Mannheim Road and become a caring and loving stepmother to the four-year-old JBP.

Below: Whetley Lane Elementary School. Following a bad attack of measles young Jack began his formal education at Whetley Lane Infant School of which his memories were not good. The headmistress and Jack's father did not see eye to eye and she took an instant dislike to his young son. 'I remember my own terror and despair at an age… when you feel small, helpless and apparently doomed, arriving day after day with fear curdling your inside.'

Left: Cricket in Manningham Park, *c.* 1904. Early in his life JBP possessed a love for the outdoors and the open countryside. At that time open fields adjoined Mannheim Road and the wide open grassy spaces of Manningham Park were not too far away for a game of cricket.

Below: Saltburn United. JBP loved soccer, from taking part in 'impromptu' matches with his street friends from Saltburn Place on the open land adjoining Scotchman Road, to the West Riding County Amateur League as a teenage member of the Toller Lane Tykes team. Here young Jack (striped shirt, back row) turned out at full back for Saltburn United at Moorfield Park on 5 May 1905.

Right: Map of Saltburn Place/Mannheim Road. Amy Priestley gave birth to a daughter in November 1903, a step-sister Winnie for young Jack. The enlarged family, following Jonathan's promotion to the headship of a new elementary school nearby at Green Lane, Manningham, moved just around the corner from Mannheim Road to 5 Saltburn Place.

Below: 5 Saltburn Place was a much more spacious house laid out in the grounds of Moorfield, formerly the estate and home of Bradford textile magnate Edward Priestman. In his book *The Edwardians* (1970) JBP describes the house as having 'a kitchen where we ate when we were by ourselves; a front room where we ate when we had company; a smaller and gloomier back room … a bathroom on the half landing, two bedrooms and two attics. The front attic was my bedroom from the first and afterwards …my "den". The house, solidly built of stone cost about £550'.

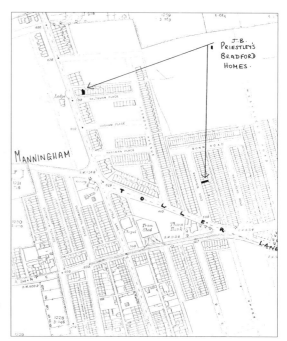

Cartwright Hall, Lister Park, Bradford was only a brisk walk or a short tram ride from the Priestley home, this building and its grounds in the summer of 1904 provided the venue for the Bradford Exhibition, one of the greatest events in the city's long and proud history. For young Jack the memory of that summer was with him for a lifetime. In 1951 he recalled: 'My playmates and I in our new suburb about a mile away from the park and looking down on it we lived like young gods … just to know it was there … and merely behind some railings was happiness'.

Industrial Hall, Bradford Exhibition, 1904. This housed an impressive range of Bradford textile goods as well as up-to-date textile technology. Jack Priestley borrowed a 400-page catalogue (price sixpence) which offered him 'a purely objective glimpse of the Industrial Hall' but perhaps signalling his own short career in the textile business six years later. There was also a Concert Hall.

Above and below: More popular with the masses were these two features at the Bradford Exhibition: the Water Chute (above) and the Somali Village (below), 1904. For Jack and his friends, atop a mill yard wall for the six-month duration of the exhibition, there was also a twice-weekly firework display 'whistling rockets up in the night sky, all in the pure ecstasy of boyhood'.

Somali Village. Washing Day.

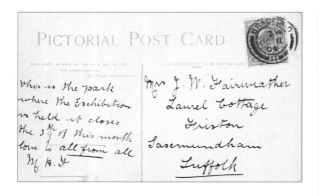

Above and opposite: Playing out. Despite his father's status and reputation as a strict headmaster and disciplinarian, JBP followed the maxim 'All work and no play make Jack a dull boy'. This was one Jack who was not going to be a dullard. He joined in the rough and tumble of schoolboy life with snowball fights in Manningham Lane against boys from the Bradford Grammar School, built bonfires on spare land, played twenty-a-side football in the fields adjoining Saltburn Place and threw himself into the 'daily scuffles in the dark sheds' of the school playground. At that time his friends probably called it 'laikin aht'.

Top left: Postcard from the Exhibition, October 1904. The Exhibition months (May–October) coincided with a hot and sunny summer. Visitors, like the writer of this card, came from far and near. By the end of the event 2.5 million people are said to have attended. For young Master Priestley, living on the very doorstep, it was a particular 'delight'. 'The vividest memory I have of the Bradford Exhibition of my boyhood, better even than the water chute or the Somali village or the fireworks, is of the Fairy Fountain which changed colour to the waltzes of the Blue Hungarian band…'.

Above left: Ally Sloper's half holiday. Inevitably, in a house stocked with books and magazines of all kinds, JBP was going to be a keen reader and as a young boy this was an early favourite comic. In time, Richard Pendlebury, his English teacher (and personal friend of Jonathan Priestley) steered him to more serious works. JBP once wrote that 'I wrote many an essay for him, knowing even then that his praise and blame alike were pure gold'.

STREET

Belle Vue Higher Grade School, 1905. At the age of eleven Jack Priestley became a pupil at Belle Vue Boys Preparatory School where his father had taught only two years earlier. By 1907 he had qualified for a scholarship to the Boys' High School in this same building in Manningham Lane.

> Mr Priestley has been appointed Head of the Evening School. He leaves on Friday.
>
> Sept 5. New No. for School of Science 5351 received.
>
> " Mr Marsden returned this afternoon after 2½ days illness.
>
> School of Science report from Board of Education 1901 – 1902
>
> This is an excellent type of a Higher Grade School. The instruction throughout is of a sound practical character, well adapted to the requirements of the Students. The

Extract of the Inspector's Report on the School, 1902. The school was one of several higher-grade schools which had developed quite naturally out of Bradford's successful elementary Board School system. Sheffield and Leeds Boards had similar institutions. Under headmaster Richard Lishman, Belle Vue Boys School acquired a nationwide reputation for its science teaching. Incidentally this log book entry also shows that Jonathan Priestley had accepted an earlier promotion as head of the Belle Vue Evening School prior to his move to Green Lane.

Woodwork class at Green Lane Board School, 1901. JBP was not impressed by his school's reputation for science teaching, in fact he had little time for any subjects other than English and history. Woodwork also did not appeal to him – 'how I loathed all that sawing, chiselling and filing'.

Gymnastics Club, 1911. Here the successful Bingley Parish Church Gym Club displays its trophies for the season but Jack Priestley detested gymnastics as a boy 'and I have never admired it since; those Czech mass antics seem to me a horror, halfway to the anthill'.

Headmaster and pupils of Green Lane School, 1907. Jonathan Priestley was a well respected head teacher by the parents and pupils at this school. His diminutive stature and boyish looks made him popular with his young charges throughout his teaching career.

Archaeology on Baildon Moor, *c.* 1910. At the same time however, Jack Priestley's father was able to command the respect and interest of his own two children, particularly Jack who, as a young teenager, often accompanied his father on long walks into Airedale or Wharfedale. As an amateur botanist or archaeologist there was much for Jonathan to stimulate the curiosity and interest of his son on the moors at Baildon and Ilkley. Here a small party of amateur antiquarians explore the foundations of an ancient boundary wall, possibly at Baildon.

Ben Tillett's picnic group. Following the strike at Manningham Mills in 1891, working-class deference and support for the Liberal Party in Bradford weakened and at Firth's Temperance Hotel in East Parade the working men of Bradford formed a separate political organisation of their own, the Bradford Labour Union, putting forward their own candidate, Ben Tillett, for Bradford West in the general election of 1892. He was not successful but the BLU had been established as a separate political entity which was popular with new socialist supporters like Fred Jowett and Jonathan Priestley and their families.

First National Council of the Independent Labour Party in 1893. The success of the BLU confirmed its leadership of the labour movement in Bradford and Bradford was consequently the venue of the inaugural conference of this new national political party in January 1893. Here the duly elected National Council stands before the Labour Institute in Peckover Street, Bradford. Jonathan Priestley threw his political weight behind this growing socialist movement. After the Manningham strike he fully sympathised with the demand for independent working-class political representation.

Above left: Fred Jowett, *c.* 1946. Priestley senior canvassed for Jowett in the municipal election of 1892 when a young Fred Jowett reminded his working-class supporters that whether 'their rulers are Liberal or Tory, they are capitalists first and politicians afterwards'.

Above right and opposite: Socialist Sunday school. The ILP provided a whole framework of leisure, education and entertainment to get its socialist message across. Rambling groups, cycling clubs, a cricket league, all made a contribution. Jowett, a personal family friend of the Priestleys, had formed the Bradford Labour Church as early as 1891 presenting the moral gospel of socialism. In the first of these two images is another big name from the socialist hall of fame. Vic Feather stands here on the East Bradford Socialist Sunday School processional cart as it begins its traditional journey on Bradford's May Day parade in 1925.

(j)   SOCIALIST TEN COMMANDMENTS : These would be fixed to the walls of the
                                 Socialist Sunday Schools which emerged
                                 during the 1890s.

SOCIALIST
TEN COMMANDMENTS.

1.—Love your School Fellows, who will be your fellow workmen in life.

2.—Love learning, which is the food of the mind; be as grateful to your teachers as to your parents.

3.—Make every day holy by good and useful deeds and kindly actions.

4.—Honour good men, be courteous to all men, bow down to none.

5.—Do not hate or speak evil of anyone; do not be revengeful, but stand up for your rights and resist oppression.

6.—Do not be cowardly. Be a friend to the weak and love justice.

7. Remember that all the good things of the earth are produced by labour. Whoever enjoys them without working for them is stealing the bread of the workers.

8. Observe and think in order to discover the truth. Do not believe what is contrary to reason, and never deceive yourself or others.

9. —Do not think that he who loves his own country must hate and despise other nations, or wish for war, which is a remnant of barbarism.

10.—Look forward to the day when all men will be free citizens of one fatherland, and live together as brothers in peace and righteousness.

Left: Diamond Jubilee Fire at Great Horton, 1897. In 1889 Bradford had become a county borough and eight years later to mark the golden jubilee of the town's incorporation the council asked the Queen to grant city status upon the old Yorkshire township. Her approval meant the people of Bradford had cause to enjoy a double celebration in the summer of 1897, beginning with this huge bonfire at Reevy Beacon.

Below: Diamond and Gold Procession, Bingley Main Street, 1897. The city celebrations of 1897 were a public demonstration of a community that was moving with great self-confidence towards a new century and an even higher level of civic and municipal development. By 1900 socialist pioneers were on the move in Bradford with a vision of municipal socialism that was to reach into so many areas of public concern, including a public water supply for all.

Scar House Reservoir, Nidd Valley, 1936. Thirty miles from Bradford in the upper reaches of Nidderdale, lay the answer to Bradford's chronic water supply problem. Two giant lakes were to be created in order to provide 2,200 million gallons of fresh clean water per year. In 1904 the first sod was cut at Angram Reservoir and shortly afterwards Scar House reservoir was completed. In the process of building both over many years, a self-contained village of over 1,000 inhabitant navvies and workmen was allowed to sprawl over the side of the remote dales valley.

Angram Reservoir, 1904. Here the first sod is cut at Angram in the Nidd Valley by Alderman Holdsworth, Chairman of the Bradford Water Committee. This and the later Scar House Reservoir assured Bradford ratepayers of a reliable supply of clean water for the foreseeable future.

Opposite above: School meals, 1908. In the years before 1914 Bradford socialists were particularly proactive in the field of educational welfare. Medical supervision of schoolchildren began in 1893 and the first school baths were opened at Wapping in 1899. Subsidised feeding of needy Bradford schoolchildren had taken place since 1892 but not until 1907 did the new Bradford Education Authority provide school meals for poor children out of the public rates. Eventually a central cooking depot was built alongside Jonathan Priestley's school at Green Lane. Here the small team of kitchen staff stand proudly over some wholesome-looking meat and potato pies.

Opposite below: Breakfast at Green Lane, 1907. At the start of each day poor and undernourished children were served a simple hot drink, bread and jam and an orange by Mr Priestley (without apron) and his deputy before school lessons began.

Weighing a pupil at Green Lane, 1908. J.B. Priestley in a preface to Fred Jowett's biography in 1946 wrote: 'it was at my father's school that the first children in this country received school meals and we knew all about it at home because this piece of social service, considered a revolutionary step then, attracted a good deal of attention in both the local and national press with the further result that photographs of my father weighing some children were widely published'.

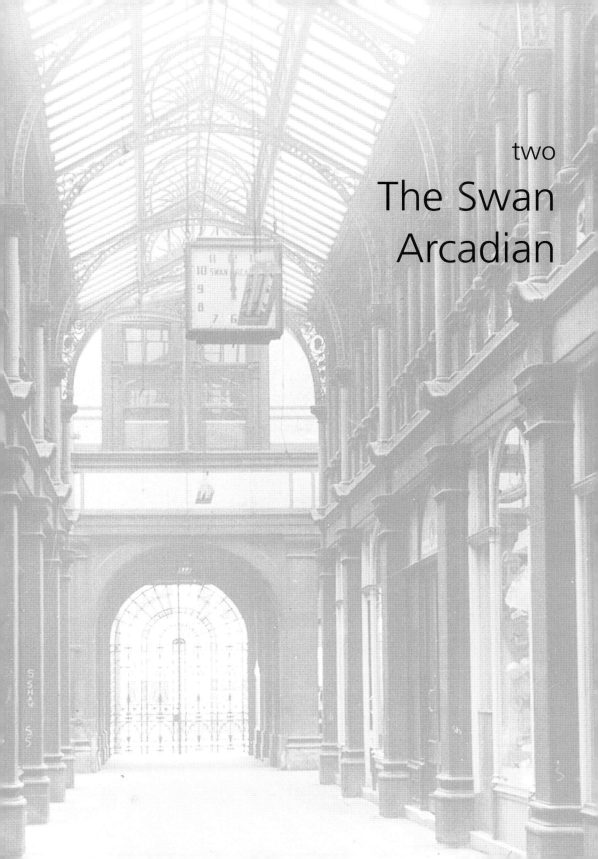

two

The Swan
Arcadian

Above: Bradford Park Avenue FC, 1908. By the age of sixteen Jack Priestley had the makings of a good footballer. His lifelong friend Percy Monkman thought him 'a solid and very good full back'. He played for his school team in that position and in 1911 he was given a trial by the town's most recent professional club, Park Avenue, which had only recently been admitted to the Southern League (1908) and played their games on the former rugby ground in Horton Park Avenue. Priestley failed to impress the Park Avenue coaching staff. Perhaps the FA Cup triumph of Bradford City in 1911 had inspired the young teenager from Manningham?

Left: Moorside, Baildon Moor, *c.* 1900. All members of the Priestley family enjoyed the great outdoors and as he grew older Jack Priestley continued to take advantage of the wonderful countryside and open moorland on Bradford's doorstep. Camping on the moors and roaming the local dales was a weekend treat or holiday pastime with his friends or family. This small upland community at Moorside, Baildon, was a favourite Priestley spot to visit.

Dick Hudson's, *c.* 1900. A threepenny tram ride (to Arcadia!) took father and son to Bingley and a stiff uphill walk via Eldwick to the edge of Ilkley Moor brought them to Dick Hudson's, a favourite pub, famed for its ham and egg teas and roast beef lunches.

Bradford Public Library, Kirkgate, *c.* 1890. Another favourite highlight of the Priestley family's social calendar included Saturday morning shopping trips to Kirkgate Market and a visit to the public library next door.

Left: Lister Park bandstand, *c.* 1914. In summer, the family would promenade around the brass band concerts on Saturday and Sunday afternoons. By the age of sixteen (in 1910) Jack, as a red-blooded young male, had his own agenda on these occasions, as Lister Park was a favourite venue for meeting young ladies.

Opposite: Mabel Sealby, *c.* 1907. Priestley wrote in 1974, aged eighty, that he was in love with two different goddesses, the girl next door aged thirteen and Mabel Sealby, principal girl in the Bradford Theatre Royal pantomime of 1905. He saw her only the once with his family, never wrote to her, never hung around the stage door, 'But her saucy black curls haunted me … every time she was mentioned in our local press, her name blazed out at me'.

Below: Unknown girl on Shipley Glen, *c.* 1910. As a youth Jack Priestley was attracted to pretty girls; in love with at least three in his final year at school. He once walked across Bradford and back one Sunday evening just to catch a glimpse of a girl at a Methodist chapel service.

Above: Working Women's Group, Eastbrook Hall, 1908. Edwardian beauties like Miss Sealby brought glamour, beauty and not a little fantasy to the drab monotony of Bradford life, but the woman on the common Bradford scene was old before her time, with a back bent from childbearing and endless hours of domestic cleaning.

Left: Washday, *c.* 1904. One or two women became obsessed by housework. The front room was always the Sunday room when dust sheets, even newspapers, were removed. Monday was invariably washday as Priestley reminded his Home Service listeners during wartime: 'When days really were days and each had a character of its own, when I was a boy up Toller Lane, Bradford, there was no mistaking Monday. You could smell it just as you could smell Thursday which was baking day in our house. Monday, of course, was washing day. It was a day when the house was fairly lost in soap suds and steam.'

Darley Street, *c.* 1900. If Monday was washday, Saturday would invariably find Jack in the centre of the city where he visited the library and browsed in the music shops of fashionable Darley Street…

…or treated his sister Winnie to pie and peas in a cosy café of Kirkgate Market 'our nearest approach to the Oriental Bazaar'. This magnificent market building was designed by Bradford architects Lockwood & Mawson and was opened in October 1872.

Above: Kirkgate Market interior, *c.* 1900. Inside, the market was tightly packed with permanent stalls, shops without windows and 'on one side there are queer old-fashioned little eating places where you can tuck into boiled cod and steak pie sitting in pens. There are rows and rows of drapery, boot and shoe, confectionery and grocery stalls'.

Left: Leaving chapel at Eastbrook Hall in 1908. Young Jack's desperate search for a good time at weekends clashed with the keen Sabbatarianism of his father who would never buy a Sunday newspaper and argued frequently with his son about allowing the iniquities of the 'Continental' Sunday into his working life. Jack was forced by his father to attend Westgate Baptist Chapel every Sunday. Here, at the junction of Vicar Lane and Leeds Road, Methodists in their hundreds leave the Sunday morning service at Eastbrook Hall in 1908.

Eastbrook Hall Midsummer Garden Party, 1909. However the social side of chapel life – bazaars, field days, Whitsun charabanc trips – were tolerable to the lively youth, he rebelled strongly against his father's puritanical views of what to do on Sunday evenings.

Final school report, July 1910. This final school report shows that JBP, aged sixteen, went out into the adult world without school certificates or public examination successes. It also records that on leaving school he took up the occupation of shipping house clerk in the Bradford wool office of Helm & Co., a commonsense choice made for him by his father who thankfully did not force his son into slogging on for a university scholarship. 'Contrary to some reports. I have never been at any age a systematic hard-slogger.'

Left: Bishop Blaise – patron saint of woolcombers. This detail on the façade of Bradford's Wool Exchange building symbolises the importance of the wool trade to its citizens. Bradford had become the world centre of worsted cloth production which, in 1910, was the largest source of employment in the city, giving work to 27,393 men and 34,232 women. The industry continued to be run by small family firms although dominated by large family business empires like the Fosters at Queensbury, H.W. Ripley, Daniel Illingworth and S.C. Lister at Manningham.

Below: Weaving shed at Pudsey, *c.* 1890. A period of uncertainty after 1874 saw overseas competitors muscling in on traditional Bradford markets. The response from West Yorkshire mill owners was to move down the production cycle and provide these new competitors with spun yarn for their weaving sheds, and later with combed tops for their spinning frames.

Right: Helm & Co. Ltd, Swan Arcade, Market Street. Just across Market Street from the Wool Exchange was the Swan Arcade building which housed the premises of this small wool tops exporting business

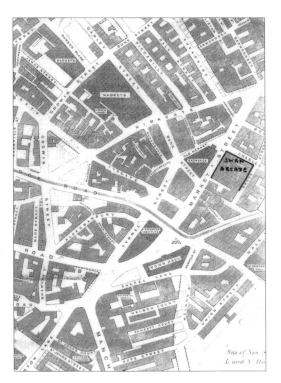

Below: Wool sorting, *c.* 1900. Priestley later waxed lyrical about the cosmopolitanism of the wool office, 'blue-wrapped cylinders of hair… Take down some of those greasy or dusty samples and you bring the ends of the earth together. This wool was lately wandering about on our own South Downs. This comes from the Argentine and this from Australia. Their adventures are terrific'.

Above: Swan Arcade interior, *c.* 1960. The contempt Priestley held for the dullness of his work as a junior shipping house clerk was not matched by his feelings for the building in which he was employed. The premises of Helm & Co. were several floors up the majestic Swan Arcade built in 1879 and a giant among English shopping arcades at the time. The five-storeyed building of glass skylights and ornamental ironwork fascinated the young man who loved to mooch and meander around its shops, stalls and kiosks. In 1962 JBP gave a personal and detailed account of this impressive building in his autobiographical book *Margin Released* where he described himself as a Swan Arcadian condemning the 'glass and concrete monotony' which had replaced the arcade when it was demolished that year and in spite of his very personal public protests.

Opposite above: Wool conditioning house, *c.* 1902. In 1891 the Bradford Chamber of Commerce had suggested some kind of testing centre for checking the moisture content and other properties of raw wool. The first venue for this was at the rear of the Town Hall but in 1902 it was transferred to Cape Street off Canal Road. JBP made numerous visits to this building and to the company's warehouse in Little Germany. Both provided opportunities for smoking a pipe of his favourite Cut Black Cavendish which he bought for 3½d from Briggs' tobacconist shop on the Market Street side of Swan Arcade.

Opposite below: Wool warehouse, Little Germany, *c.* 1900. Helm & Co.'s office, according to JBP 'was an entirely masculine office without a touch of feminine grace and light … it was in fact dull. I much preferred the atmosphere of the firm's warehouse half a mile away where the wool arrived to be sorted.'

Above: Lyons Tea and Coffee House, Market Street, *c.* 1895. After work, JBP spent a lot of his leisure time at the Joseph Lyons tea shop round the corner from work in Market Street (on the extreme right of this photograph can be seen Lyon's well known gilded shop sign over the entrance). Inside, the café was long, dark and narrow with an upper level.

Below: Young men relax after work in Bradford, 1905. 'Sometimes on winter evenings bound afterwards to a play or a concert … we golden lads … made straight for the upper level, the back room you might say, where we were capable of monopolising a couple of tables for hours while spending about sixpence' on coffee and a poached egg on toast.

St George's Hall, *c.* 1890. JBP
played the piano in the family
home at Saltburn Place and loved
the music of Wagner, Beethoven
and his favourite, Brahms. All
were played by the Halle and
London Symphony orchestras
which were frequent visitors to
this public concert hall in the
years before the First World War.
Priestley's favourite conductors
were Richter and the dynamic
Nikisch. Leaving the shilling
gallery he 'would come reeling
down that long stone flight of
stairs, drunk with the music, my
head starrier than the night'.

Prince's Theatre, Little Horton Lane, *c.* 1890. This small theatre shared this site with the Peoples' Palace
(formerly the infamous Star Music Hall). The entrance to the music hall was down the side street on
the right of the photograph. During the twentieth century it premiered several of J.B. Priestley's early
plays and was a favourite with the writer and with many of Bradford's theatre-going public until its
closure in 1961. In Priestley's younger days it staged light-hearted melodramas which incurred the
wrath of Priestley senior who even frowned upon his son's visits to the more serious stage dramas at the
Theatre Royal and positively raged at Jack's playing truant from night school to take in the first house
at the Empire Music Hall.

Empire Theatre, Great Horton Road, *c.* 1914. One of the Edward Moss chain of variety theatres, this had opened its doors in 1899 and was built on to the rear of the licensed premises of the Alexandra Hotel. Knockabout comedians, female impersonators and pretty lady ballad singers entertained both the rough and the respectable of Bradford's theatre-going public. As a young man Jack Priestley enjoyed its fourpenny balcony though these were 'not the cheapest seats as there was a twopenny gallery behind us – where I forgot my discomfort – the expert packers treated us like sardines'.

Alhambra theatre site, 1914. John Rand's mill was demolished in 1913 to create this empty plot which one year later became Francis Laidler's Alhambra variety theatre. The Empire and Alexandra Hotel can be seen to the right and came off second best in the competition for customers during the First World War. Priestley's favourite Empire theatre finally brought its curtain down on the music hall era when a serious fire damaged much of the building.

'Little Tich', *c.* 1900. Real name, Harry Relph and one of young Priestley's favourite knockabout comedians. 'The matter of his songs and sets was the old traditional stuff – mother-in-law, the lodger, kippers and beer, dubious sausages and dangerous cheese, an ancient round of japes', all rounded off by his gestures, oversized boots and his droll and diminutive appearance.

Vesta Tilley. Priestley barely tolerated male impersonators but he favoured Vesta Tilley as the best of them. He was however impressed by a little redhead called Maidie Scott. His favourite male comedians were Harry Tate and George Robey and the relatively unknown Jimmy Learmouth – 'one of the best comics I ever saw who drank hard and died young'.

Horace Healey's Symphonic Jazz Band, *c.* 1932. This is the only period photograph of a Bradford jazz band I was able to access but Priestley himself tells us that jazz had arrived in Bradford long before the First World War: 'One evening, hot and astonished in the Empire, we discovered ragtime … We were used to being sung at in music halls in a robust and zestful fashion but the syncopated frenzy of three Americans was something quite different; shining with sweat, they almost hung over the footlights defying us to resist the rhythm … what we were hearing for the first time was Alexander's Ragtime Band.'

A visit to Scandinavia, June 1913. Priestley's lazy and casual attitude at work, and his foppish and outlandish clothes, did not endear him to his employers, though he was competent and worthy enough for an all-expenses-paid business trip to Denmark and Sweden in the summer of 1913.

J.B. Priestley and his attic 'den' at Saltburn Place, 1970. Even before he had left school Jack had decided to become a professional writer. His moderately successful school newspaper and the constant encouragement of Richard Pendlebury fixed his resolve. In 1911 a humorous London weekly magazine had accepted one of his literary efforts and by 1912 he had already cultivated a small circle of journalist friends at Lyons. Despite the usual tensions of family life (between father and teenage son) Jack Priestley continued to live at Saltburn Place, but once he had climbed the attic stairs 'and closed the door behind me I was no longer a junior wool clerk, I was a writer – poet, story-teller, humorist, commentator and social philosopher, at least in my own estimation'.

Left: Bradford Pioneer, March 1913. Since the beginning of that year, Priestley had contributed regularly to the columns of the town's socialist newspaper, the *Bradford Pioneer*, edited by Alfred Pickles.

Below: Round the Hearth, June 1913. This was JBP's column in the paper, a weekly review of the Bradford cultural scene 'journalism of the humblest sort and unpaid at that'. The rest of the paper was narrowly and fiercely political. 'My father and many, though not all of his friends, were socialists. They were not Marxists – and I doubt if there was a student of economics amongst them – they were all in the looser and warmer English tradition of socialism'. At least this regular column gained him free access to local theatres and music halls and concert venues.

BRADFORD PIONEER, FRIDAY, JUNE 13, 1913.

It must be distinctly understood that "Round the Hearth" is pre-eminently a personal feature, so that the opinions expressed therein are not necessarily those of the paper itself. Letters dealing with subjects treated in "Round the Hearth" are invited, and should be addressed to, "J. B. P. c/o BRADFORD PIONEER."—ED.

Children's Competition.

After carefully reading through the many essays I have received in con-

you can make yourselves? Often when reading a poem happy thoughts seem to flit everywhere, all your dull thoughts seem to disappear. Often that same

Keep your eyes open for another co petition and better luck next time.

The Bradford Playgoers' Society.

This Society held its first ann meeting in Channing Hall a short ti ago. The room at the Arts Club lately proved to be too small for meetings and readings and the co mittee has decided to use Chann Hall next winter. The first open reading took place some weeks ag the grounds of the Myddleton Ho Ilkley, and the experiment was an qualified success, partly due, proba to the play chosen—"Prunella," delightful fantasy by Lawrence H man, and Granville Barker. Mr. Lishman has been elected chairman the Society for the next season, an

Wool clerks, *c.* 1920. As a junior wool clerk Priestley was not the office boy though occasionally he did have to fill inkwells, put out blotting paper, operate the copying press and 'take enormous bundles of wool samples to the General Post Office, a chore I particularly detested … I felt my golden youth was slipping away'. It is not hard to see why there was a cultural optimism about Bradford at the turn of the twentieth century, a culture that was similar to that of Liverpool in the 1960s. For all its provincialism Bradford was international – even cosmopolitan – in its outlook, the wool trade had seen to that.

Deutsche Evangelische Kirche, Great Horton Road.

And then there was this curious leaven of intelligent aliens, chiefly German-Jews and mostly affluent. They were so much a part of the place when I was a boy that it never occurred to me to ask why they were there. I saw their outlandish names on office doors, knew that they lived in certain pleasant suburbs, and obscurely felt that they had always been with us and would always remain. That small colony of mixed or foreign Bradfordians produced some men of great distinction, including a famous composer, two renowned painters and a well known poet.

Prior to the outbreak of war one of the best known clubs in Bradford was the Schillerverein. In *English Journey* J.B. Priestley wrote that 'there was then this odd mixture in pre-war Bradford. A dash of the Rhine and the Oder found its way into our grim runnel – "t'mucky beck". Bradford was determinedly Yorkshire and provincial, yet some of its suburbs reached as far as Frankfurt and Leipzig. It was odd enough but it worked'.

three

Off to War

Ambitious to succeed as a professional writer and living in a vibrant and progressive city at the forefront of social reform and cultural diversity, it was inevitable that the routine and narrow monotony of a wool office would not hold Jack Priestley for ever, but it was events well beyond Bradford and out of his personal control which finally persuaded him to make the break and leave the city.

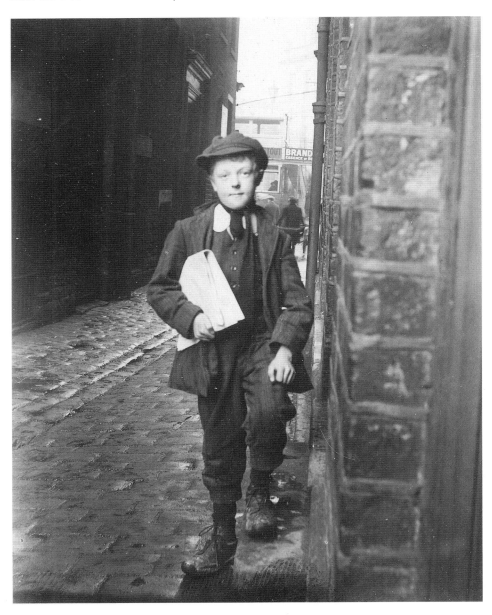

Bradford news boy, *c.* 1904. In August 1914, as the countries of Europe stumbled and blundered one by one into war, young Jack Priestley was alone at home when he heard the news of the declaration of war. Mother and father and sister Winnie had gone for a holiday to Blackpool but he waited until September before joining up.

Blackpool and its tower, *c.* 1900. The annual Priestley family holiday was normally to Scarborough but the ladies of the house favoured Blackpool and the Lancashire coast, well served by regular excursion trains from the city's Midland Railway station, particularly on the August of Bowling Tide week. Blackpool's tower was completed in the year of JBP's birth (1894). Here a Fleetwood fishing smack sails along the Blackpool seafront to serve a new and more lucrative tourist need. It was from one of these early fishing families, the Bickerstaffes, that the enterprise and initiative came to build Blackpool's tower. Using the tightest of budgets John Bickerstaffe and his brothers finally opened the 510 feet high tower in 1894. The base of the tower housed an aviary, aquarium, menagerie, and later a circus, all for wet weather entertainment.

Left: Infantryman J. Priestley, 1914. By his twentieth birthday, 13 September 1914, Jacky Priestley had signed up with the Duke of Wellington's West Riding Regiment, known across Yorkshire then as the 'Havercake Lads' or the 'Dirty Dukes'. He had already reached the first major crossroads of his life. It was time to leave behind Swan Arcade, Market Street, Bradford and Saltburn Place, Manningham.

Below: JBP's postcard to his family in 1915. During a fortnight of intensive training at the regimental barracks in Gibbett Street, Halifax, Jack Priestley was allowed home each night to sleep. Most of his friends had volunteered for the Bradford Pals battalion at Belle Vue Barracks, Manningham, a circumstance in his favour in July 1916 when all but 200 of 2,000 Bradford Pals were slaughtered on the Somme battlefield. However by the end of September 1914 he was transferred to Frensham Camp near Aldershot with the rest of his platoon (No. 8) B Company 10th Duke of Wellington's 69th Brigade, 23rd Division. Before leaving for Frensham he had sent his family copies of the previous photograph of a newly promoted lance corporal.

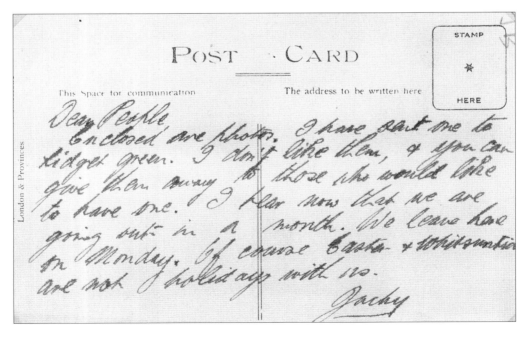

Above: Route march, 1914. This Bingley scene was being repeated all over urban and coastal England in 1914. Following a Christmas at home with his family, Priestley's platoon was, in February 1915, transferred to Aldershot and then route-marched to Folkestone, a hundred miles away, with people waving and cheering along the route. Prior to his posting to France, Priestley was made Battalion Post Corporal.

Right: Typed letter home from Bramshott Camp, August 1915. As the rest of his family holidayed in Llandudno that year, Jack Priestley was still training in England. He had already lost several of his old Bradford pals in France and was well aware of the slaughter and carnage on the other side of the Channel.

on YMCA paper

Bramshott Camp
Aug.2 - 15

Dear People,

In your last letter you didn't enclose the cutting from the "Telegraph", but I chanced to see a copy of the "Weekly Tele" & therein found the account of Day's death in the firing line. Through Foster, I knew him quite well; he was one of our Lyons cafe habitues & a frequent visitor to the "Camp". Intellectually, he was not so brilliant as the appreciation in the "tele" made out he was, but, nevertheless he was a fine fellow, an upright & clearminded Englishman. He was the idol of his parents & sisters; it must be a fearful shock to them.

Aug.2nd ! & still in England ! How the time passes on. It strikes me that they will need a great many more men in France shortly, so perhaps we shall go there. I hope so. The men here are getting thoroughly dissatisfied at being kept so long training & training month after month, & there are many slight signs of disturbance, so much so that the discipline is being made much stricter, heavy packdrill being given to defaulters. Of course we are being trained to do things that were not dreamed of in modern warfare a year ago. & when we do go, we shall not go to our slaughter as the Regulars did, but properly equipped with machine-guns, machine-rifles (the new invention) & bombs of every dexription. Hope you are enjoying yourselves at Llandudno, & wish I could spend a day or two with you, but "no go".

Jack

Goods Yard, Midland Railway station, Bradford, 1914. Bradford was one of the first towns to form its own Citizen's Army of Volunteers following the declaration of war. This Bradford battalion, with its headquarters at the skating rink in Manningham Lane, drilled in local parks with obsolete rifles. Here, the battalion (Bradford Pals) prepares to leave Bradford for Liverpool docks for Marseilles via Egypt and ultimately for the Somme.

```
                              Dec 24/ 15
Dear Ma,
     We have left the trenches & their environs for about a
fortnight. Dad wrote asking me to get something for Winnie,
but I wasn't able to get anything at the time because I
wasn't anywhere near a town, & in any case, I hadn't any
money. You will find enclosed a fancy handkerchief (typically
French), which I bought for Winnie last night. For your
information, it comes from a little town only three miles
from the trenches, a little town that is often shelled by
the Germans. If I could have got to one of the larger towns
further back I could have got some very pretty "souvenirs",
though they are very expensive.
     This is Westgate paper. I received the parcel the other
night, & a very fine parcel it is too ! I wrote to Mr Ransford.
By the way, what's that white powder in the tin box ? Is it
tooth-powder, baking-powder, plug of tobacco, cigarettes, matches,
what ? I have seen some of the Bradford parcels, though I
haven't got mine yet. All our chaps are laughing at them.
The whole contents aren't worth sixpence. Halifax has sent
us a splendid parcel each, containing candles, a tin of toffee,
a cake, a plum pudding, plug of tobacco, cigarettes, matches,
& a large tablet of toilet soap. Huddersfield sends us
cigarettes regularly.
     The rain it raineth every day, here; it knocks Bradford
into a cocked hat. With best wishes for the festive season !
          Yours affectionately,
                    Jack
```

Left: Typed letter to his step-mother, Christmas Eve, 1915. By this date Jack was a veteran of trench life and night raids into no-man's land, but still grateful for the variable quality of parcels from home. His father obviously had no idea of the terrible conditions his son was having to endure; reminding him to buy a Christmas present for little sister Winnie. Earlier that month Jack had lost his best friend Irvine Ellis. The two men had enlisted together, trained together and would have died together had Jack not been summoned further up the line at the time the shell had exploded. 'Irvine's cheery companionship', he told his father 'had helped to lighten many a dark hour.'

Opposite above: O.T. Camp in North Wales, 1916. Within a year of leaving England Jack Priestley was wounded at the Western Front. The large trench mortar which buried him alive left him partially deaf. He was transferred to a military hospital in Leicester where he was visited by his parents. Once on the mend, he was transferred to Hambleton Hall, a Georgian country house converted into a convalescent home. Eventually passed fit, he joined the 2nd Battalion of the 96th Brigade for training in the OTC in North Wales. With them he is seated here on the second row from the front (with stick). From there he was assigned officer class to the Devonshire Regiment and sent back to France.

2nd West Riding Regiment in the front line, 1918. Here, in the Oppy-Gavrelle sector, two men clean and maintain a Lewis gun and behind them a young soldier watches the enemy front line through a box periscope. In the autumn of 1916 JBP returned to the front line only to be gassed and declared permanently unfit for active service. He was discharged from the army in 1919 more fortunate than many of his boyhood peers.

Left: Private J.E. Armstrong, aged eighteen, was one of those less fortunate than Priestley. Armstrong spent his early years as an orphan in the Keighley workhouse; worked at Low Mill, Keighley from the age of twelve and took the king's shilling aged sixteen. A hard, short and brutal life snuffed out on the Western Front.

Below: Priestley's boyhood, *c.* 1900. In 1933 he wrote: 'there was a gang of us, went "chumping" just before 5th November, played "tin-can squat" and tally-ho round the half built houses, climbed and larked about on the builder's timber stacks, exchanged penny-dreadfuls and sometimes made plans for an adventurous future.'

Above left: Hargicourt Cemetery near Rousel, France. Priestley continues:

> *They were all sent to the attack on the Somme on 1 July 1916, when they were butchered with remarkable efficiency … There are great gaps in my acquaintance now and I find it difficult to swap reminiscences of boyhood. 'The men who were boys when I was a boy' the poet chants; but the men who were boys when I was a boy are dead. Indeed, they never even grew to be men. They were slaughtered in youth; and the parents of them have gone lonely, the girls they would have married have grown grey in spinsterhood, and the work they would have done has remained undone.*

Jack Priestley left the army in 1919 'with a chip on my shoulder; a big heavy chip, probably some friend's thighbone'.

Above right: 'They pass and smile, the children of the sword.' In 1933 Priestley attended his first battalion reunion at the Market Tavern, Bradford. Of this occasion he wrote: 'I had seen the dead more often than the living. And I think that if, when I climbed the stairs of this tavern, I had seen my friends Irvine Ellis, Herbert Waddington and Charlie Burns waiting at the top, grinning at me over their glasses of ale, I would not have been shocked nor even surprised.'

Left: Back home from the Front. Like many officers who had survived the carnage, Priestley returned home reluctant to talk about his war experiences though they must have taken their psychological toll (he never lost his fear of travelling on the London Underground). Five months before the armistice, Priestley's school teacher hero and personal friend to his father, Richard Pendlebury, was killed in action at the age of forty-eight.

Below: An attic office, 1911. Back home at Saltburn Place in a saddened and sombre city, Priestley climbed the steps to his den and quickly resumed his writing career with a guinea a day commission from the *Yorkshire Observer*'s editor in Bradford, to write a series of articles on a walking trip around the Yorkshire Dales. Writing under the pen name of Peter of Pomfret, his column became popular with many local readers who took their country walking very seriously.

A Yorkshire Dales cairn, *c.* 1900. 'We were all great walkers then with the best walking country in the world so close; before the motor car had taken over.' Most northern mill towns had some kind of 'escape route' to a nearby rural retreat. Bradfordians looked to Wharfedale or the Aire Valley and the wooded attractions of Shipley Glen. Some walked collectively, even competitively, but most, like this group, struck out on their own.

Left: J.B. Priestley with his first wife Pat in 1914. Within a short time of his return from the war he began courting Pat Tempest, the daughter of a Manningham neighbour.

Below: Reading Room, Bradford Library, Kirkgate. Here Pat Tempest worked as a librarian throughout the war years. She had corresponded with JBP during the whole of that time and visited him at Hambleton Hall. Perhaps it was expected of him that he would marry her for marry her he did on 29 July 1921, at Westgate chapel just round the corner from the library.

Cambridge University, 1921. By that year Jack had received a services' grant to study history and political science at Trinity Hall, Cambridge. Determined to realise his career as a writer, he and Pat set up home in a flat at Walham Green, London, where he augmented his income as a proof-reader for a publishing house. He never again lived permanently in Bradford.

Statue of J.B. Priestley overlooking central Bradford.

Market Street, Bradford, *c.* 1900. As he went off to London to become a literary giant of the twentieth century, his Bradford life came to an end. He returned only as a visitor but no one thinks of him without thinking of Bradford. That 'go ahead', progressive, pioneering, reforming city shaped his formative years and influenced much of his later writing, existing as a real social and cultural world, yet offering him a spiritual vision for which to live, an inspiration from which to create and to write:

> *Still, I passed the first nineteen years of my life in the north and those are the years that count. I was moulded and coloured so to speak by the West Riding and more particularly by Bradford … And I'd have you know that Bradford of those years was no ordinary city. … I tell you Bradford was quite a place in those days and I am prepared to bet that it produced more well-known people, musicians, scientists, writers, performers and the like than any place anything like its size in the whole Kingdom. It was a rattling good environment for any youngster.*

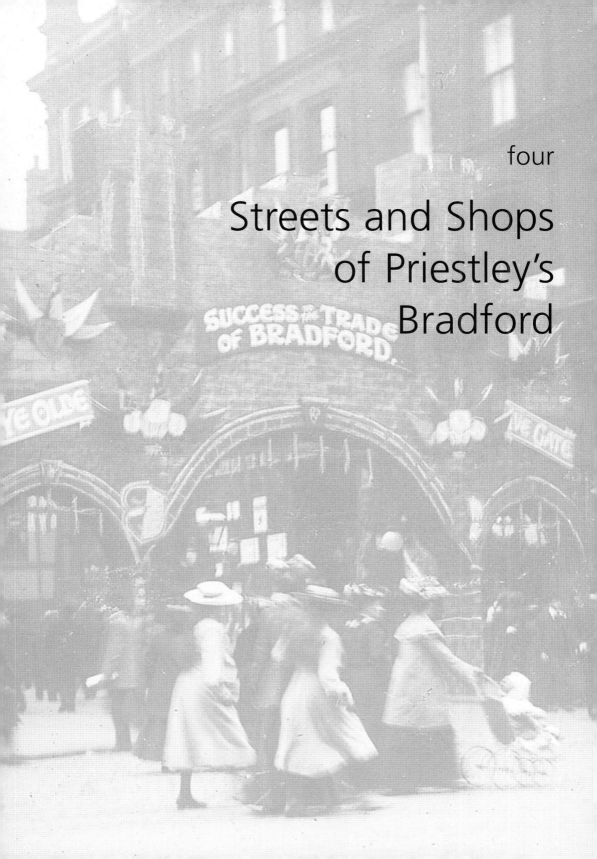

four

Streets and Shops of Priestley's Bradford

Bird's eye view of central Bradford in September 1899. This is a detail from a town map of Bradford reproduced in the *Warehouseman & Draper* of September 1899 and therefore technically Victorian.

In the top right-hand corner is the medieval core of the ancient township around Kirkgate, Ivegate and Westgate. The first addition to that came as late as 1782/3 when New Street (later Market Street) was constructed.

Thereafter, and in line with the town's population and commercial growth after 1801, an early warehousing precinct emerged alongside Kirkgate, Piccadilly, Dale Street, Duke Street and Cheapside. In the bottom right-hand corner of the map is the terminus and station of the Midland Railway, rebuilt in 1882 but first opened in 1846. This created a new urban focus around the Midland station and hotel at what was to become Forster Square (formerly Bermondsey and Cheapside).

At the centre of the map, highly valued land in Hall Ings belonging to Charles Swaine Booth had been sold for warehousing in 1837 and laid out in a grid formation, putting an end to the old 'Broad Stones' route to the church. Between 1840/70 Charles Street had become a busy highway for wool men linking the Wool Exchange in Market Street to their home trade warehouses in Peel Place. This was a new 'triangular square' created by the junction of Leeds Road and Hall Ings.

After 1830 mill owners and manufacturers set the pace of Bradford's urban growth with their need of waterside mill properties and warehouses for their finished goods. As a result some ancient family estates disappeared. Charles Harris sold part of his Eastbrook House estate for warehouses in Well Street (bottom left) and the rest was laid out for warehouses by Thomas Dixon after 1856 to create a commercial zone which later came to be known as 'Little Germany'.

In the top left corner of the map much of the land is taken up by Bradford's other railway. The Lancashire & Yorkshire Railway finally got round to building a new station in 1885/8, ignoring the pleas of Bradford businessmen to link up with the Midland Railway. Completed in 1888 this new station of ten platforms cost £300,000. The one advantage of this 'white elephant' of late Victorian Bradford was the simultaneous construction of the Great Northern Hotel (the Victoria Hotel) in Bridge Street at a time when the town was chronically short of first class hotel accommodation.

Forster Square and Midland station, *c.* 1890. Midland Hotel at rear.

Demolition of housing in Bermondsey to accommodate the new Midland station.

Peel Place (*c.* 1885) dominated by the statue of Sir Robert Peel, founding father of English free trade. Home-trade warehouses complete the scene.

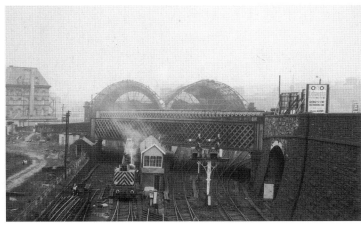

GNR and LYR railway station built in 1885/8.

Old Crown Hotel, Ivegate, *c.* 1906. An ancient hostelry in one of Bradford's oldest streets. Its tiny rooms, low ceilings and narrow corridors gave way to accommodate a music hall. Here Bill Richardson stands at the door to the dram shop which he had converted from one of the pub's saloon bars. Next door but one on the right is Tommy Wardle's hardware shop.

Kirkgate, *c.* 1890. This busy retailing sector was popular with the Priestley family each Saturday morning. To the right is the popular entrance to the Kirkgate Market (built 1866-71), a favourite with most Bradford shoppers at the turn of the twentieth century. In the centre is the large tea warehouse of Brooke, Bond & Co.

Westgate 1891. Looking towards the junction of Kirkgate with Ivegate. Walker & Sons in the distance also marks the junction with Millergate. On the right are the premises of the famous Bradford jeweller, Fattorini & Co.

Westgate, *c.* 1890. Another view of Westgate at about the same period but looking west towards North Parade and Manningham Lane. On the far right is the Central Hotel (formerly temperance) and adjoining it is the relatively new shopping emporium of Lingards.

Left: Lingards interior, *c.* 1938. A favourite inter-war store with housewives and housekeepers but best remembered for its overhead automatic change dispenser from each counter assistant to a central cashier point in the centre of the store.

Below: Kirkgate Market building, *c.* 1895. Following the purchase of the medieval manorial market rights in 1866, the council built this magnificent building (now no more and its demolition vehemently opposed by JBP in 1972). Priestley was not on his own, as 25,000 Bradfordians urged the council not to demolish it. It had opened in October 1872. To the right is Darley Street and on the corner is Leuchter's Restaurant, famous for its hosting of the oyster supper in April 1890 when the Barbarians Rugby Club was founded.

Ivegate, *c.* 1904. Ivegate's status as a main street of Bradford was in the doldrums for much of the nineteenth century. Shoppers ignored it because of its steepness and narrowness. The Victorians had made few improvements to its ancient character and yet here it proudly boasts a toast to the success of the trade in the town. In Priestley's day it was dominated by pubs, music halls and pork shops and it was to these that young men like JBP were drawn for a good Saturday night out in the early years of the twentieth century.

Forster Square, *c.* 1900. W.E. Forster had been MP for Bradford when he passed the important Education Act of 1870 on behalf of a reformist Liberal government. In doing so, he created a national system of elementary Board Schools which lasted until 1902. After 1890, when his bronze statue was unveiled by the Marquis of Ripon, this area of Bradford became a new urban focus of the increasingly prosperous and successful town. It became a popular terminus for the new corporation tram system with a landscaped area around Forster's statue in the centre of the roundabout. Here the GPO building, much visited by the young wool clerk, is on the left and the export wool warehouses of Well Street act as a backdrop to the square.

Forster Square, *c.* 1900. This time looking up Bolton Road from the Post Office corner. On the left are two council cleansing carts keeping the square free from horse droppings.

Forster Square, *c.* 1920. After the First World War the square became a proper travel interchange for Bradford commuters, particularly for the local corporation tram services. Forster's statue remains but Oastler's had been relocated by this time.

Forster Square, *c.* 1910. At the opposite end of the square was this more popular statue of Richard Oastler, friend to the factory children. Erected directly opposite the main concourse of the Midland Railway station, this was the first sight which greeted and inspired Margaret McMillan, on a rain-soddened night like this in November 1893. She brought her gospel of socialism to the Bradford School Board and introduced educational welfare measures like school baths, meals and medical inspections, all of which the Priestley family approved.

Town Hall Square, *c.* 1890. The grandeur and openness of this area in front of the Town Hall is affirmed in this photograph by the lack of any public transport and by the enormity of the façade of the Mechanics Institute building (1871). In the foreground is Bridge Street.

Town Hall Square, *c.* 1905. The square as J.B. Priestley knew it, busy, uncluttered and a proper civic and municipal heartland.

Town Hall Square, *c.* 1945. By this time, and hardly known by JBP, the square had become a public transport nightmare. The electric tram is still in use but so is the motorbus and trolleybus. At centre is Burton's, the gent's outfitters, and left is Halford's bicycle shop.

Bridge Street, *c.* 1900. To the right is St George's Hall and looming large in the central distance is the Mechanics' Institute. Queues for trams (right) only became a feature of Bradford streets after the introduction of electric traction in 1898. Hitherto there were no official stops.

Above: Market Street, *c.* 1910. Jack Priestley's favourite Bradford Street. The camera is pointed towards the Town Hall with the Wool Exchange and Hustlergate at right centre. On the left are wool offices and half-way down on the left was Swan Arcade.

Left: Town Hall Square/Market Street, *c.* 1895. The bow-fronted building (left) at the end of Market Street is the George Hotel where mine host was Tommy Wood. Horse and cart was the main means of transport at this time when Emma and Jonathan Priestley were first getting used to parenthood.

Manningham Lane, *c.* 1895. The photograph is dominated by the Yorkshire Penny Bank (centre) built in that year. To the right of the bank is North Parade recently created as a result of the extension of Darley Street. The horse-drawn tram passes the entrance to the Theatre Royal (left) and Royal Arcade (right).

Manningham Lane, *c.*1900. Another view of this busy approach road into Bradford from the west. The photographer is probably located at the front of the Yorkshire Penny Bank with Manor Lane to his right and North Parade to his left. The building with the large flag pole is the Royal Arcade better known to Bradfordians in the inter-war years as Busby's department store but not really known to a young Jack Priestley.

Busby's first store, c. 1908. He may however have known Ernest Busby's bow-fronted double shop façade on Kirkgate which had opened as a general drapery in 1908. By 1930 Busby was joined by his three sons and they purchased the Royal Arcade premises on Manningham Lane for their new department store.

Windhill Co-operative Society, c. 1900. Department stores like Busbys and Brown Muffs were probably beyond the economy of lower middle-class families like the Priestleys. As committed socialists they probably did much of their shopping at the local co-op. The Windhill Cooperative Society had been founded in that part of the outskirts of Bradford called Windhill as early as 1864. In their first year they were able to pay a dividend of 2s 3d in the pound and they prospered thereafter with premises all over the Bradford district. This is the grocery and general hardware store at Baildon Bridge. I am sure many of the older generation of Bradfordians can still remember their Co-op check or divvi number!

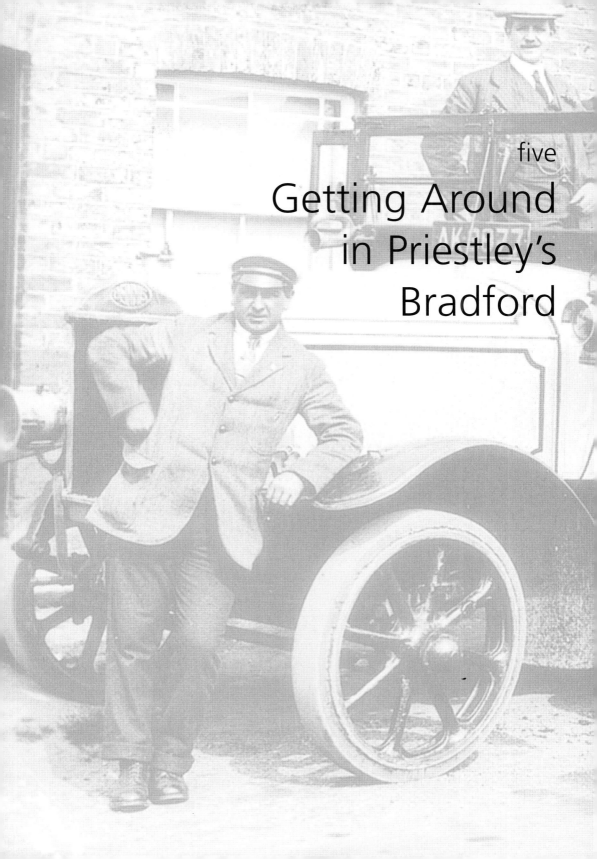

five

Getting Around in Priestley's Bradford

This Edwardian street scene reveals the variety of ways of getting around Bradford at that time. Prior to the age of the motor car most people travelled by 'shank's pony' or bicycle, apart from horse owners in the countryside. JBP once reminisced in the columns of the local press that the Bradford he knew as a boy was small and compact enough 'to walk clean across and back one Sunday evening just to catch a glimpse of a girl at a Methodist chapel service'.

Except when the weather was very bad, people walked everywhere, saving pennies and walking for exercise. This was not a keep fit campaign, simply a cheap and convenient means of transport, of getting around.

Cottingley Toll Bar, *c.* 1913. This symbol of the turnpike era of the eighteenth century survived into the twentieth. Here a local farmer walks his cattle to market taking a route that Jonathan Priestley and his son, Jack, knew well as they rode by tram from Saltburn Place then walked via Cottingley into the open countryside of Airedale or the upland moors of Baildon.

Sunday school field day at Shipley, 1912. Hundreds of Shipley Sunday school scholars congregate in the local market place for the traditional Whit Monday Walk from their respective schools to this mass gathering, where church leaders and a portable harmonium lead the hymn singing.

Above: Country walking for all the family, *c.* 1906. As soon as you wanted some real walking you turned your back on Bradford and made for the moors like this Bradford family, the Bowers, who have rested on this limestone outcrop in Craven.

Opposite above: Heading for the hills. Jack Priestley later confessed that on a fine spring or autumn morning he would occasionally not walk towards Market Street and the tedium of his Swan Arcade office but go in the opposite direction and head for the open countryside.

Opposite below left: The Bradford Whit Walk. Some even took their walking so seriously they became quite competitive about it. A tradition of competitive road walking was begun in Bradford in Jack Priestley's youth. Since 1903 the city had been the headquarters of the County Walking Association and in that year hosted its first Whit Walk when a crowd of thousands surrounded the George Hotel in Market Street to see the start of a forty-mile race, taking in Otley, Tadcaster and York. Baildon's Len Atkinson, wearing rubber pumps, won that first race in just seven hours and seven minutes.

Opposite below right: Two winners of the Bradford Whit Walk. T. Lloyd-Johnson (177) of Leicester won the race twice in the early 1930s. On the left (49) is J.W. Joy of the Wibsey Park Athletic Club. He came first in the Bradford to Settle race in 1927.

BRADFORD & COUNTY WALKING ASSOCIATION

(Founded 1903)

President: H. W. RAISTRICK, N.C.A.A.

69th ANNUAL

BRADFORD WALK

UNDER A.A.A. LAWS & R.W.A. RULES

DISTANCE: 50 KILOMETRES
(31 miles, 121 yards)

also incorporating the

NORTHERN AREA RACE WALKING
ASSOCIATION CHAMPIONSHIP
at this distance

**Starting at 9.30 a.m. prompt
from New Bank Street, Bradford
on MONDAY, 31st MAY, 1971**

Longbottom's Smithy, Bingley, 1912. Unfortunately for those who could afford to keep a horse to get about, the days of horse-drawn transport were numbered. For three centuries the Longbottom family had shoed horses on this site only to surrender the property to an entrepreneur of the moving pictures business. Within a year, this ancient smithy had been replaced by the Hippodrome cinema.

Charabanc trip, c. 1890. Before the era of the bus, coach and car, these horse-drawn charabanc trips to the seaside and countryside were popular with young people of Jack Priestley's generation. He was well familiar with them, as his Uncle Tom (Holt) was landlord of the Volunteer public house in Green Lane, Manningham, and he frequently organised holiday or weekend charabanc trips like this one.

Bradford Canal, *c.* 1930. The introduction of canal transport after 1770 revolutionised the movement of heavy goods and materials. The route of the Bradford Canal (1774), which ran three miles north from the centre of Bradford to join the Leeds-Liverpool Canal at Windhill, was almost redundant by 1894 when Priestley was born. However, here at Windhill as late as 1930, coal is still being loaded into barges travelling into the city.

Leisure boating at Bingley on the *Alexandra*, *c.* 1895. One of several steam-driven pleasure crafts owned by the Leeds-Liverpool Canal Company. Here the boat has just ascended the Five Rise Locks and heads west past Bingley's Elizabethan manor house of Gawthorpe Hall.

Left: The coming of the railways to Bradford. Bradford men of commerce were slow to seize the opportunities offered by the railway revolution. Bradford was located in a small blind valley off the main line which was always a problem once Leeds had set the pace. Bradford's first railway in 1846 ran from central Leeds along the Aire Valley to a Market Street station. The Lancashire & Yorkshire Railway (LYR) had opened a line from Halifax via Low Moor into Drake Street station in 1850 while two years later the Great Northern company ran a line from Leeds to Adolphus Street station.

Below: Midland Railway station, *c.* 1890. By 1871 the Market Street station had become part of the Midland Railway which opened this six-platform station in 1890 with a terminus hotel to follow soon after.

INTERIOR,
MIDLAND RAILWAY STATION,
BRADFORD.

Exchange station, 1960. In 1867 a branch line ran under Wakefield Road and joined the LYR at Mill Lane, allowing Great Northern trains into Drake Street station, or Exchange station as the enlarged station became known. The joint railway companies finally got round to building a proper station in 1888 at a cost of £300,000.

The Exchange station, 1970. This new station of ten platforms was covered by two 100 feet arched roofs. Bradfordians might remember a heavy stone-built bastion hidden from public view by numerous wool warehouses, its steep and dismal pedestrian staircase was another forgettable experience.

Above: Great Northern Railway, Caledonia Street Crossing, *c.* 1870. A Lancashire & Yorkshire Railway locomotive halts beside Waterloo Mill in the vicinity of Manchester Road, Bradford in the 1870s. As the train halts at Caledonia Street Crossing (left and distant) a railway official closes the gate for road traffic. The locomotive is heading south and has probably left Drake Street station, or Exchange station as it became.

Left: Trams in Sunbridge Road, *c.* 1919. For those who could afford it and for those unable to walk, the city's system of tramways was the quickest and cheapest way of getting around Bradford. On his way to work, Jack Priestley took the 'Duckworth Lane tram to its terminus at the bottom of Sunbridge Road (as here) and then walked along Market Street to Swan Arcade pretending to be a junior clerk in a wool office'. The Bradford corporation trams system had evolved since the 1880s.

Horse-drawn street car, Manningham Lane, *c.* 1885. For those Bradford citizens without their own carriages, this service between Darley Street and Lister Park had been available since February 1882. It was run by a private company which leased the track from the council. Worn-out cab horses, ready for the knackers yard, were used and often collapsed dead in the street.

Steam tram at Frizinghall, *c.* 1800. The public demand for a faster and more widespread system of public transport forced the corporation to introduce steam trams in the 1880s. At 12mph they were considered by some to be too fast and certainly too noisy.

Above: Steam tram and trailer at Saltaire, 1895. Staff and engines outside the maintenance sheds, Exhibition Road, Saltaire.

Left: Electric trams reach Saltaire, 1902. The council had experimented with electrically driven trams as early as 1883 but did not run them in the city centre until 1898. Here, the service along Manningham Lane has been extended to Saltaire at an official opening in Gordon Terrace, April 1902. The introduction of this service gave the Priestley family another option for escaping their city to the green fields of Airedale.

Above: First trolleybus at Laisterdyke, 1911. The council introduced the trackless trolleybus to its citizens three years before Jack Priestley went off to war.

Right: Toller Lane tram in Duckworth Lane. However the first trolleybus route from Laisterdyke to Dudley Hill had little relevance for him as his memories were always of the 'stately swaying galleons of the Toller Lane tram'.

Bradford tram accident, July 1907. Trams were not without problems; this accident occurred with a runaway tram on the notorious incline of Church Bank. There were no fatalities here as the accident happened early in the morning when passers-by and passengers were few.

Arrival of the motorcar, c. 1900. This coincided with Jack Priestley's early years. Although private cars were few on Bradford roads prior to 1914, commercial delivery vehicles like these began to appear.

School meal deliveries, *c.* 1906. Even school meal deliveries were made by lorries. According to his son, Jonathan Priestley was easily annoyed by the loss of privacy that lorry drivers caused him at Saltburn Place, 'always jumping up from the dinner table to dash out and remonstrate with them'.

The transport fleet of Lister & Co., *c.* 1914. Parked at the rear of Manningham Mills and at the base of the mill's giant chimney, this was the transport available to Lister & Co. at the time of the First World War.

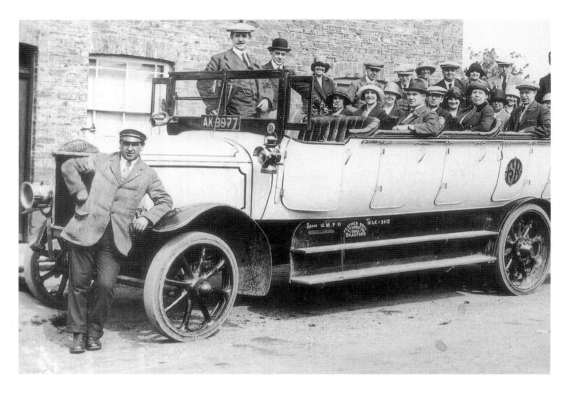

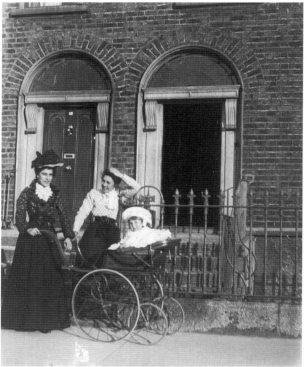

Above: Charabanc trip, *c.* 1920. The internal combustion engine also transformed Uncle Tom Holt's charabanc trips from the Volunteer public house in Green Lane. Excursions could now go all the way to the seaside and back in one day. Feather Bros were running daily excursions like this until well into the 1960s.

Left: Perambulator, *c.* 1900. Moving babies and young children about the city was also no longer a problem to the late Victorian middle classes.

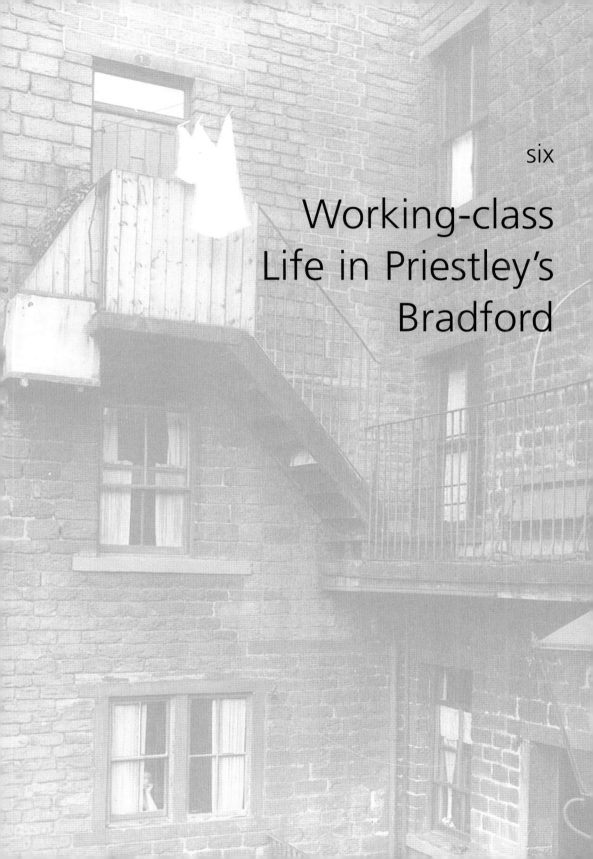

six

Working-class Life in Priestley's Bradford

With both sets of grandparents coming from the ranks of the working class, and encouraged by his father to mix with boys whose parents were 'back o't mill', it is little wonder that JBP understood throughout his long life that the kind of people who appear in the photographs of this section of the book were among the 'salt of the earth. They ought to have been sluts and brutes but they were not – they were decent and kind, humorous and hopeful, often responding eagerly to any faint gleam of beauty, a song, a sunset, a handful of wild flowers'.

Well into his fifties Priestley was still fighting their corner. Never a card-carrying member of the Labour Party, he felt, even after 1945, that the war against social injustice was still to be waged. If his father had taught him anything, it was that the prosperity and success of the Bradford trade in the nineteenth century had been brought about by people who went 'clattering to work so early in the morning, through dingy little back streets to huge dark mills'.

It was their nimble fingers, tired eyes and aching backs that produced the mansions and grouse moors and yachts and hot houses, the silks and peaches and cigars and old brandies. I realised early as a boy that you were lucky to get any more than would keep you barely alive, if you toiled day and night at the combing machines and the looms.

Opposite: A backyard near Leeds Road, *c.* 1904. Families, little better off than each other, came to the help of neighbours when times were hard. It was easy for women and neighbours to become friends, living so close to each other.

Right: 'Popping next door', *c.* 1900. There were very few secrets between neighbours because you could often hear everything through house walls and anyway that kind of privacy was never understood because everybody was the same.

Below: Back-to-backs in Woodend, *c.* 1900. 'Toilets were outside, not the modern ones of today. They were the old types and emptied once a week.'

Opposite above: Work people's housing, *c.* 1914. As late as 1921 when Priestley had returned from the war, Bradford still had 41,000 back-to-back houses (54% of its total dwellings). 3,700 were considered unfit for human habitation but were still lived in. So much for 'homes fit for heroes'.

Opposite below: The Landings at Windhill, *c.* 1940. The author remembers these homes still inhabited as late as the 1950s.

Right: The living room, *c.* 1900. This single room on the ground floor of a back-to-back house in Victorian Bradford, served both as kitchen and parlour. The baking bowl on the table would suggest it was Thursday, always baking day in the Priestley home. The bareness of the room contrasts sharply with a …

Below: … middle-class drawing room of the time with its fussiness and clutter.

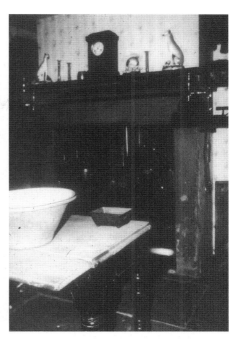

Opposite above: Kitchen range, *c.* 1900. The coal-fired boiler and cooking range (left) took up the whole of one wall in a Bradford back-to-back but it provided hot water as well as heating for most of the house.

Opposite below: The 'cellar-head'. The main water supply, from a single cold tap, was usually found in the Bradford back-to-back at the top of the cellar steps set back from the living room.

Right: Bawdy mill girls, *c.* 1904. Occasionally, when JBP finished earlier than usual at Helm & Co.'s office, he would walk home and his preferred route took him past Drummond's mill gate just as the shift was finishing. 'I would find myself breasting a tide of shawls and something about my innocent dandyism would set them screaming at me and what I heard then, though I was never a prudish lad, made my cheeks burn.'

Below: Mill's out, *c.* 1900. Young women leave their work behind for another day, hooded in their shawls for the walk home. Above a certain age, to be seen in public uncovered, provoked street gossip and a reputation for indecency.

Family fortunes, *c.* 1900. Contrasting fortunes in these two photographs. *Left:* A family of three await the arrival from work of their breadwinner father. *Below:* An evicted family, deserted by the father, was not too far away from the workhouse. The mother, aged before her time with continuous childbearing, had few prospects of becoming a wage earner overnight.

Mother's ruin, 1904. From the outdoor department of Mr Popplewell's off-licence shop in Seymour Street, a respectable housewife secretes a jug or bottle of something beneath her pinafore for private consumption back at home.

Boys will be boys, Leeds Road, 1904. Most boys of the lower working class held part-time jobs long before they left school. As unofficial errand boys they gathered round tram stops, railway stations, large hotels and corner shops. They fetched and carried for building labourers, shoppers, and hotel porters. They earned important shillings for the family income.

'Taws', *c.* 1900. A break for two Bradford errand boys with a game of 'taws', marbles or glass alleys. There is no reference in the Priestley family archives of young Jack running errands for money although I am sure he must have played a mean game of marbles at one time or another.

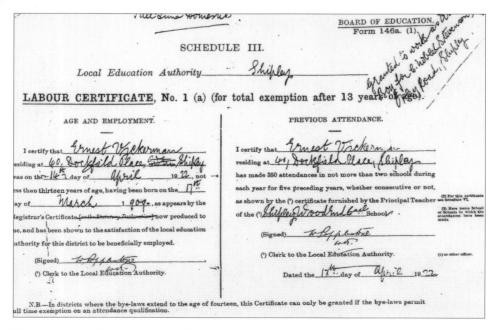

The Labour Certificate, 1922. From the late 1880s School Boards became more tolerant as they relaxed the law on compulsory school attendance. Under pressure from local mill owners, children were allowed to be exempt from school after the age of thirteen, if regular work was guaranteed and educational standards had been reached. Here, Ernest Vickerman has been granted his certificate as a full-time domestic worker/errand boy.

Right: Matriarchy, Leeds Road, *c.* 1900. Here, a matriarchy holds sway during the daytime of Bradford's working-class back streets and courts. Mothers presided in judgement over the behaviour of their children, decided upon the expense of the next family meal, undertook the round of household chores or relaxed with a neighbourly gossip.

Below: Mount Street, Bradford, 1904. By the time of JBP's departure from Bradford, the acute poverty of early Victorian times was in retreat. For this neighbourhood gathering in 1904, times are probably still very hard but they are well clothed and seem healthy despite posing outside the tobacconists and Mr Ellis' pawnshop.

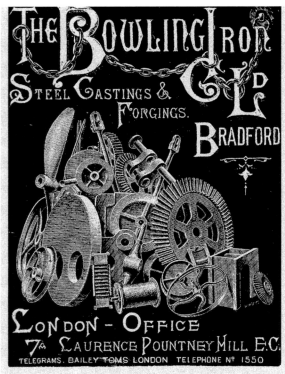

Advertisment from ENGINEERING dated Sept.1st 1893

Left: Bowling Ironworks, 1893. In the previous photograph there is a distinct absence of adult males. After textiles, the second major employer of Bradford male labour in 1871 was iron manufacture (1,411), although this was a long way behind the 38,000 men employed in textiles. Bowling Ironworks had opened in 1788, thrived in Victorian times, and became a limited company in 1870. By the time of this advertisement the company was in terminal decline and closed for business in the following year.

Below: Coal digging at Bradford Moor, c. 1926. Industrial relations were poor after the First World War and frequent strikes in the coal industry forced men and women onto the spoil heaps of former coal pits like this one at Bradford Moor.

seven

Leisure Time in Priestley's Bradford

Eastbrook Mission Hall, 1905. The pressure on Bradford working men to find sober and respectable leisure pursuits came from a variety of evangelical groups like the temperance movement, Band of Hope and these members of the Eastbrook Hall Methodist congregation whose Reverend H.M. Nield mounted a vigorous outdoor public campaign of missionary work in the summer of 1905. He must have had some success as several Bradford publicans demanded of the council a reduction of their rates on the grounds that the 'Eastbrook Brotherhood had robbed them of their customers'.

The sports and pastimes shown in this section of the book are largely those of the popular leisure which occupied the middle and working classes of Edwardian Yorkshire. For most of the nineteenth century the battle to win the minds and the leisure time of men and women had been taken up by the traditional adversaries of pub versus church, brewery versus chapel.

Prior to 1800 there had been a seasonal round of festivals and pastimes rooted in the ancient agrarian calendar. The coming of heavy industry and the movement of large numbers of people into expanding industrial towns like Bradford, reduced the amount of free time and the number of open spaces. Both of these are crucial prerequisites for the way people enjoy themselves at any one time in history.

In northern England some simply bucked the system and went absent from work each Monday morning (St Monday), particularly in the south of the county, in Sheffield and Barnsley. Others turned to more rational forms of recreation, steered by advocates of the Evangelical movement. Temperance coffee houses, circulating libraries and subscription concerts were all expressions of this rational recreation. They all offered activities of a respectable and improving nature in order to deflect popular culture away from the evils of drink and the dangers of the crowd.

By the middle of the 1800s, economic and political forces were at work to stimulate a trend towards the use of mass leisure pursuits particularly after 1870. The railway revolution of the 1840s had made the coastline available to all if only as an annual day excursion. More enlightened factory legislation freed up the Saturday half day which meant a window of opportunity for any leisure activity. Society was changing sufficiently for the better, to create a context in which traditional games and recreations, as well as new, could become organised nationally with an efficient centralised body of officials, skilled players and thousands of eager spectators across the land. Most of our mass sports of today were shaped in this period: the Football Association (1863); Yorkshire County Cricket Club (1863); Yorkshire RFU (1888). Young Jack Priestley was born into this surge of competitively organised spectator sports.

Above: Beehive Inn, Westgate Bradford, *c.* 1890. In spite of the best efforts of church and chapel, drink remained an integral part of working-class culture and the corner street public house became a feature of working-class community life after 1870. This was a popular pub in the city centre but particularly with Bradford's large Irish community.

Below: Royal Standard Hotel bar, *c.* 1900. This saloon bar was popular with the Bradford theatre-going public who attended at the Theatre Royal's semi-serious dramas next door.

Above: Bradford Theatre Royal, October 1905. The Royal Standard Hotel is here sandwiched between the theatre and the Masonic Connaught Rooms. This photograph was taken by the repertory theatre's manager the day after Henry Irving's death on Friday 13 October 1905. Completing his performance of 'Becket' with the final lines of the play 'Into thy hands O Lord. Into thy hands…' the Victorian stage superstar staggered off and was taken by cab a few hundred yards to his suite at the Midland Hotel where he collapsed and died in the foyer. Here, the following day the theatre flag is at half-mast, the billboards have been blanked out and Irving's business manager Bram Stoker is about to cross the road (with umbrella) having announced the sad news to the rest of the company.

Right: Bradford Rugby Club win the Yorkshire Cup, 1884. In West Yorkshire it was amateur rugby which set the pace of mass spectator sport in the 1880s, attracting large crowds and fanatical supporters. Here, the weekly newspaper (issued each Saturday) could not wait until after the game but celebrates victory (in a very upbeat style) on the morning of the actual match.

Above: Professional rugby at Park Avenue, 1904. By this time rugby had professionalized following the creation of the Northern Union in 1895. Here, Bradford are at home to local rivals Wakefield before a capacity crowd. Professional soccer had also appeared in Bradford in the early years of the new century. Bradford Park Avenue in 1908 played in the Southern League and Bradford City joined the Football League in 1903. After only eight years City had beaten Newcastle in the final of the FA Cup before a crowd of 137,000 over a replayed final. As a sports-mad youth of seventeen, Jack Priestley thrived on their success and dreamed of life as a professional footballer, finally getting a trial at Park Avenue at the age of sixteen.

Opposite below: Spotted House, 1895. This ancient farmhouse had been a feature of the Lister estate in Manningham Lane before it became part of the Keighley, Bradford turnpike road (1825). Originally known as the Listers' Arms, it was sold to John B. Tankard in the 1870s. By the time of his death in 1894 he had added a bowling green, tennis courts and a swimming pool. The Airedale Cycling Club obviously met there in 1895 and twenty years later, each weekend Jack Priestley chose to walk to either the Black Swan at Frizinghall or the Spotted House (as this had become known) where he met friends from the Bradford Arts Club. It was advertised in the year of this photograph as a 'suburban house of refreshment'.

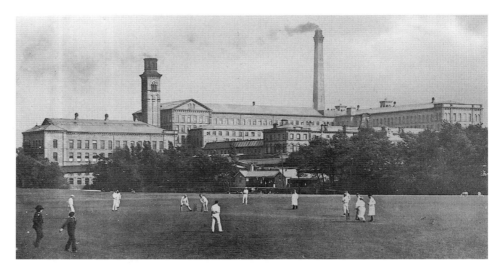

Saltaire Cricket Club, 1916. Cricket also had a strong following particularly after 1908 when the Yorkshire team triumphed in the county championship for the twenty-fifth time under the captaincy of Lord Hawke. At local level, amateur cricket reached a high standard in the Bradford Cricket League. The Saltaire Club (founded in 1865) was a founder member of that league and here play a match in wartime when support was inevitably low.

Beside the sea, Blackpool, c. 1895. Commercially motivated railway companies were quick to see the advantages of passenger transport to the seaside which became an attraction for all classes (resistible only by society's poorest). Perhaps the crowds of northern mill people or the brashness of its attractions deterred the Priestley family from visiting Blackpool. They preferred the slower pace of Scarborough or Llandudno.

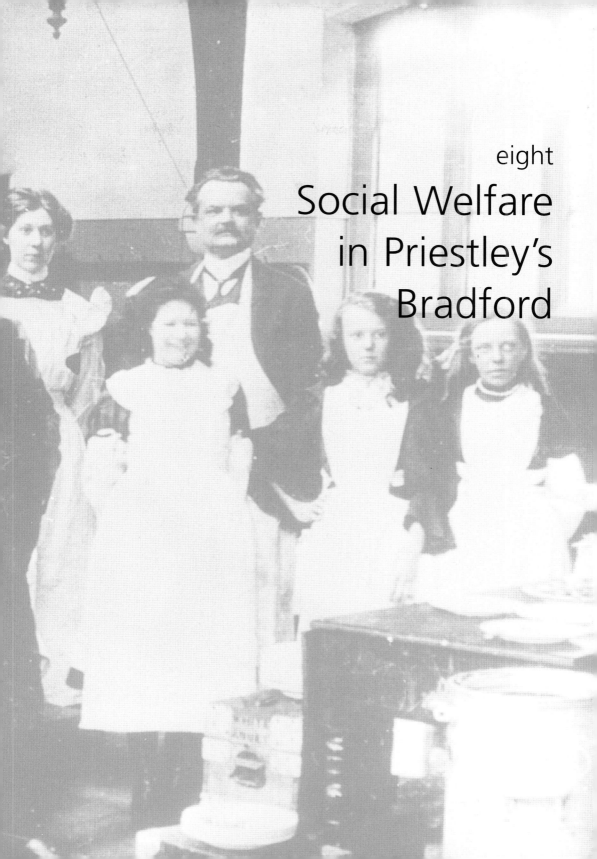

eight

Social Welfare
in Priestley's
Bradford

The fervent support of the Priestley household for the new Independent Labour Party was rewarded by that group's rapid development across the city. By 1893, it had over 2,000 members in nineteen clubs, as well as the backing of the Bradford Trades Council (unions). It had contested parliamentary elections in the city and in January 1906 returned Fred Jowett as Member of Parliament for Bradford West. However it was in the arena of local politics that it had its greatest effect and its widest influence. Although the Labour group numbered only ten out of eighty-four councillors and aldermen on the Bradford council in the years before 1914, they made, with some Liberal support, a significant and widening impact on the social welfare role of the Bradford municipal authority.

Nowhere was that impact better felt than in the field of educational welfare. In the two decades before the First World War Bradford established a reputation for proactive local government and initiated a number of policies to improve its younger citizens' standard of living. The Education Act of 1902 transferred responsibility for education from the School Boards to the local council in the shape of the Local Education Authority (LEA), which considerably increased the opportunities of ILP councillors in the fields of education and public health.

As early as 1893, local medical practitioners were pressing the Bradford School Board to appoint a medical officer for its schools. The Board had already begun classes for blind and deaf children at Carlton Street School in 1885. The far-sighted and progressive Bradford School Board also approved the provision of school dinners during the winter months by the voluntary charity of the Cinderella Club, which provided 343,741 meals in its first year (1904/5). Thus, long before the 1902 Act and the creation of the LEAs, the Bradford School Board was looking well beyond its remit of simply providing sufficient school places for its children.

Margaret McMillan first became an elected member of Bradford's School Board in 1894 when she was appalled at the condition of school children in the city's poorer districts. She attended a medical inspection with the Board's first school medical officer Dr J. Kerr, and went on to campaign for school baths, school meals and regular school medical inspections. She was an early advocate of nursery education but her ideas in this field were not taken up in Bradford until 1919.

Other examples of Bradford's enlightened policy of municipalisation in this period included the council's purchase of a private gas company; the acquisition of a reliable water supply and the reputation of the first town in Britain to possess its own supply of electricity (in 1889).

Right: W.E. Forster. He was Member of Parliament for Bradford in 1870 when he steered through Parliament the first effective Education Act which set up local authority school provision in the shape of School Boards. Surprisingly, after the Act, Bradford needed to build only eight new schools and by 1885 was providing good-quality elementary teaching for 24,000 children.

Below: Whetley Lane Board School. This was one of Bradford's original Board Schools and was built in 1876 at the astronomic cost of £17,000 or £24 per child accommodated (cf London £14 per child; Leeds £5 per child). This could be explained by the extra amount of original land purchased, as Whetley was extended in 1885 to meet the growing number of children, one of whom was Jack Priestley in 1898.

Cinderella Club Kitchen, c. 1892. The Bradford School Board gave permission to this voluntary charity, formed in 1890, to make free use of certain school cellars to prepare and serve dinners to necessitous children during the cold months of winter. This is probably the kitchen area at Green Lane School used for that purpose.

Above: Needy Bradford schoolchildren, 1908. Children like these of the Bradford Parish Church School made up the statistics of the Cinderella Club report of 1904 which found that 2,400 children were ill-fed in Bradford and another 2,250 were underfed. A further 3,000 children went hungry or were ill-shod (at least one child is without shoes here).

Opposite above: Infant Feeding Centre, Green Lane School. During the hard winter of 1905, the responsibility of feeding Bradford's needy schoolchildren passed from the voluntary sector of the Cinderella Club to the public purse of the Poor Law Guardians, who tried to recover the cost of meals from poor parents by taking legal action against them. Eventually in 1906 the Education (Provision of Meals) Bill became law, passing responsibility onto the LEA but supported by a halfpenny charge on the rates. Fred Jowett, MP for Bradford West, made a significant contribution in Parliament at the select committee stage of the bill.

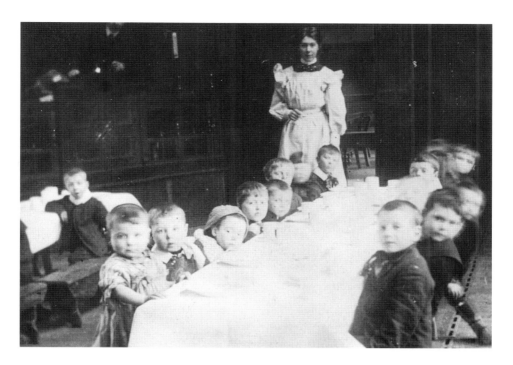

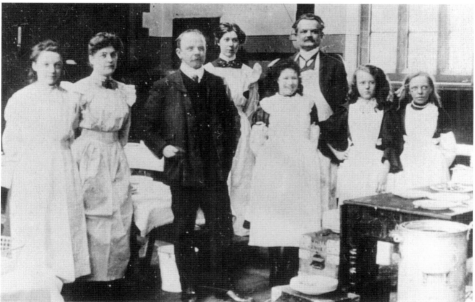

Cooking depot, Green Lane School, October 1907. Although the Liberal legislation of 1906 was permissive, not obligatory, the local ILP group made sure that the Bradford LEA adopted it by opening five feeding centres across the city at White Abbey, Carlton Street, Parish Church, St Luke's and Usher Street. A central cooking depot was also built at Green Lane School, where JBP's father was head teacher. Here, Jonathan Priestley stands proudly with his deputy and kitchen staff at the opening of the depot (first in the country), 28 October 1907, when 668 meals were provided.

Food.	Estimated quantity required.	Remarks.	Price.
Bread (Brown or White	11700 lbs.	In 6 lb long, square loaves.	per loaf.....
Flour, Seconds	11700 "		per stone....
" Wholemeal	2340 "		" "
Eggs, fresh	6500		per 50......
Milk	26000 pints		per gall.....
Beef	11700 lbs	Solid meat cut into 1 in.squares No Waste	per lb ......
Margarine	2340 lbs		per lb........
"Nutter" suet	2340 "		per lb........
Carrots	3900 "		per stone....
Onions	11700 "		"
Potatoes	15600 "		"
Turnips	3900 "		"
Fruit (in season)	7020 "		
Apples			per stone....
Bananas			per 100.....
Gooseberries			per stone....
Plums			per stone....
Rhubarb			per doz.bundle
Dates (dried)			per stone
Cabbages & other Greens			
Celery		No quantities can be given.	
Parsley			
Sweet Herbs (Mint, Thyme,etc.,)			
Lemons			
Fish	6240 lbs.	Cod,Haddock or Hake. To be ready "dressed" with no waste.	per stone....
Barley (Pearl)	1560 lbs		per stone

CITY OF BRADFORD EDUCATION COMMITTEE

EDUCATION (Provision of Meals) ACT.

FORM of TENDER for Food stuffs required.

during the year ending 30th Sept. 1908.

Left: Food stuff tender, Bradford, September 1908. Prior to the opening of the service a number of feeding experiments were carried out on forty children from two schools in the poorest quarter of the city. Much thought was given to nutritional value as well as to cost (not to exceed 2d per head). Here, the tender form for the authority's feeding needs in 1908 looks wholesome, healthy and nutritious.

Below: School meal delivery, *c.* 1908. A motor wagon, specially built for the city's steep gradients by the Bradford Tramways Committee, carried the hot food and liquids across a large area of the city. Here, hungry children await delivery of their meals at one of the dining centres, soon increased from five to sixteen.

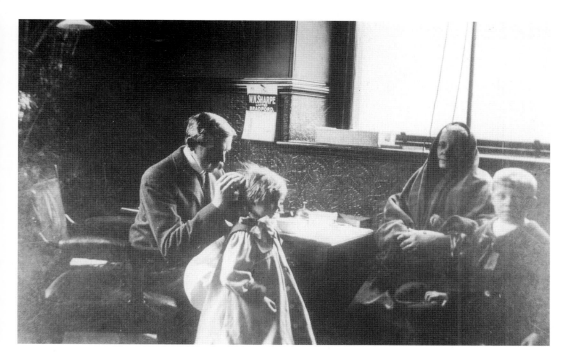

School medical inspections, c. 1900. Bradford was quick to follow the London School Board's example and appoint a Medical Superintendent of Schools in 1893, Dr James Kerr, who probably undertook the first ever school medical inspection in 1899 at Usher Street School. On that occasion Miss McMillan was in attendance when over 100 of the children had not removed their clothing for six to eight months. She immediately began a public campaign to educate lower-class parents into accepting their responsibilities, and providing public baths for those who would not.

CONCLUSION

Writing forty years after he had left Bradford, J.B. Priestley could still conjure up the sights, sounds and smells of his birthplace. There would always be a part of him in Bradford. He wrote:

> there was a centre of Bradford smell, there in Market Street except when the rains were washing it away, characteristic and unmistakeable and not acrid, not unpleasant though there was smoke and a touch of soot in it that my nose is glad to remember,

and

> But in the world outside, as I move from Stockholm, to Montreal, Tokyo to Santiago, something at the core of me is still in Market Street hearing the Town Hall chimes.

As son Tom rightly says, 'one could imagine a Bradford without him but never J.B. Priestley without Bradford'.

G. Firth
Denholme
December 2005

Other local titles published by Tempus

Bradford History & Guide

BOB DUCKETT

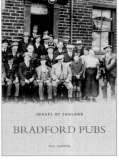

This history of Yorkshire's great textile manufacturing town of Bradford takes the reader from its earliest beginnings, through the sweat and wealth of the great industrial period to the multi-cultural, post-industrial, metropolitan borough of today. The final chapter of the book takes the form of a Walking Tour leading the reader on a journey through the modern city centre pointing out buildings and other features of the past that are still there to see.

0 7524 3702 X

Bradford Pubs

PAUL JENNINGS

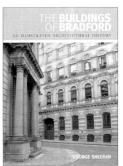

Illustrated with over 150 old photographs, plans and advertisements, this fascinating volume tells the story of Bradford's pubs over two centuries of history. The reader sees the pub in all its many guises, from the coaching inns of the early nineteenth century, to the splendid Victorian gin palaces and humble back-street beer houses, right up to the modern pubs of the twentieth century.

0 7524 33024

Buildings of Bradford: An Architectural History

GEORGE SHEERAN

Bradford has a surprisingly rich building heritage and at a time when the city is undergoing widespread regeneration with buildings of the twentieth century being demolished and earlier, often neglected, buildings restored, this book provides a timely review of significant building survivors and their place in history. George Sheeran, shows how the changing demands of population, business and industry have shaped the city's architecture and with a splendid series of photographs illustrates his historical narrative to great effect.

0 7524

Clayton

MARGARET DALGETY AND STUART DOWNEY

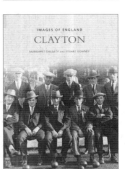

The village of Clayton in West Yorkshire has a long and proud history. This fascinating selection of over 200 archive images portrays some of the changes which have taken place in and around Clayton over the last 150 years, including the arrival of the textile industry and the village's eventual incorporation into Bradford in 1930. Shops, schools, churches and transport are all described in pictures and informative captions, as are sports teams, buildings and of course the local people.

0 7524 3701 1

If you are interested in purchasing other books published by Tempus, or in case you have difficulty finding any Tempus books in your local bookshop, you can also place orders directly through our website

www.tempus-publishing.com